<u>MORE</u> Frantic Frogs
and Other
Frankly Fractured
Folktales for
Readers Theatre

Recent titles in Teacher Ideas Press' Readers Theatre series

From the Page to the Stage: The Educator's Complete Guide to Readers Theatre
  Shirlee Sloyer

Simply Shakespeare: Readers Theatre for Young People
  Edited by Jennifer L. Kroll

Character Counts! Promoting Character Education Through Readers Theatre, Grades 2–5
  Charla Rene Pfeffinger

Sea Songs: Readers Theatre from the South Pacific
  James W. Barnes

Judge for Yourself: Famous American Trials for Readers Theatre
  Suzanne I. Barchers

Just Deal with It! Funny Readers Theatre for Life's Not-So-Funny Moments
  Diana R. Jenkins

How and Why Stories for Readers Theatre
  Judy Wolfman

Born Storytellers: Readers Theatre Celebrates the Lives and Literature of Classic Authors
  Ann N. Black

Around the World Through Holidays: Cross Curricular Readers Theatre
  Written and Illustrated by Carol Peterson

Wings of Fancy: Using Readers Theatre to Study Fantasy Genre
  Joan Garner

Nonfiction Readers Theatre for Beginning Readers
  Anthony D. Fredericks

Mother Goose Readers Theatre for Beginning Readers
  Anthony D. Fredericks

MORE Frantic Frogs and Other Frankly Fractured Folktales for Readers Theatre

ANTHONY D. FREDERICKS

Illustrated by
Rebecca N. Purvis

Readers Theatre

Teacher Ideas Press

An imprint of Libraries Unlimited
Westport, Connecticut London

Library of Congress Cataloging-in-Publication Data

Fredericks, Anthony D.
    More frantic frogs and other frankly fractured folktales for readers theatre /
    Anthony D. Fredericks ; illustrated by Rebecca N. Purvis.
       p. cm. — (Readers theatre)
    Includes bibliographical references and index.
    ISBN 978-1-59158-628-9 (alk. paper)
    1. Fairy tales—Parodies, imitations, etc.—Drama. I. Title.
    PS3606.R433M67   2008
    812'.6—dc22   2007030916

British Library Cataloguing in Publication Data is available.

Library of Congress Catalog Card Number: 2007030916
ISBN-13: 978-1-59158-628-9

First published in 2008

Libraries Unlimited/Teacher Ideas Press, 88 Post Road West, Westport, CT 06881
A Member of the Greenwood Publishing Group, Inc.
www.lu.com

Printed in the United States of America

The paper used in this book complies with the Permanent Paper Standard issued by the National Information Standards Organization (Z39.48–1984).

10 9 8 7 6 5 4 3 2 1

CONTENTS

Part I
A BUNCH OF EDUCATIONAL STUFF YOU GOTTA KNOW BEFORE YOU READ ALL THE REALLY WEIRD STUFF IN THE REST OF THIS BOOK
(a.k.a. the Introduction)

Part II
ARE YOU READY?: HERE'S ALL THE REALLY WILD AND WACKY SCRIPTS THAT YOU'VE BEEN WAITING FOR

Part III
FROG CENTRAL—A REALLY HOPPING PLACE

Part IV
STORIES THAT THE AUTHOR OF THIS BOOK DIDN'T (or Couldn't) FINISH (But Maybe You and Your Students Can)

APPENDIXES

THE REALLY SHORT SECTION THAT YOU ALWAYS FIND IN THE FRONT OF A BOOK (a.k.a. the Preface)

Once upon a time, in 1993, I wrote a book called *Frantic Frogs and Other Frankly Fractured Folktales for Readers Theatre*. That book was (and still is) a collection of really bizarre, peculiar, odd, wacky, and far-out retellings of popular and well-known children's stories presented in a readers theatre format. Some of the scripts in that book are

- "Beauty and This Incredibly Ugly Guy,"

- "Little Miss Muffet Smashes the Spider to Smithereens,"

- "Coughy, the Dwarf Snow White Never Told You About,"

- "Jack Climbs to the Top of a Very Tall Vegetable and Finds a Very Large Individual with an Attitude Problem,"

- "Rumpelstiltskin Tries to Spell His Name," and

- "Rapunzel Gets a Really Lousy Hairdo."

(As you can probably tell by now, I've got this completely and totally warped sense of humor—but let's not get into *all* my personality defects just yet.)

Anyway, that book soon found its way into catalogs, Web sites, bookstores, and lots of educational conferences around the country. It wasn't long before the book began selling "like there was no tomorrow." Teachers would buy it and use it as a major part of their language arts program. Librarians would buy it and use it to introduce familiar fairy tales and legends as part of numerous library projects.

Letters, e-mails, and personal comments I received from teachers, librarians, and kids attested to the unbelievable joy and unmatched hilarity that permeated schools from coast to coast. One teacher wrote, "My students are SO turned on to the unbelievable power of readers theatre!" Another wrote, "What a dynamic way to teach reading and all the language arts!" A fifth-grade teacher in New Jersey recently told me that she was inspired to write her own readers theatre script entitled "No Frog Left Behind—A Modern-Day Melodrama."

With the success of *Frantic Frogs and Other Frankly Fractured Folktales for Readers Theatre*, teachers and librarians would approach me during my author visits to their schools asking for another volume of wild and wacky readers theatre scripts (of course, there were others who approached me asking for small loans—but that's another story altogether). They asked (in some cases, demanded) another volume of absurd, ridiculous, and totally insane readers theatre scripts they could use in their classrooms and libraries.

Thus was born the idea for this book—a collection of MORE crazy, irreverent, demented, outrageous, gross (and other adjectives that can't be printed here) scripts that kids in grades 4–8 can use as part of their language arts program. I figured that many kids had heard of "The Boy Who Cried 'Wolf'," but how many have heard of "The Boy Who Cried 'Amphibian' (Once Too Often, I Might Add)"? Most kids are probably familiar with the version in which Humpty Dumpty fell off the wall, but never the version about him becoming a stand-up comedian. And lots of youngsters know the traditional version of "Jack and Jill" but may not be familiar with the more realistic tale: "Jack and Jill Don't Like the Stupid Author Who Wrote Their Stupid Story" (no reference, of course, to yours truly).

This is all a roundabout way of telling you how much fun I had writing the first book (and how much fun others have had using it) and how that convoluted view of traditional children's stories and fairy tale characters has been continued in the pages of this volume. I sincerely hope that you find the scripts in this book to be as welcome and amusing as those in the first volume and that they will "energize" your students with an overwhelming abundance of hilarity, humor, amusement, fun, jocularity, and infectious good times.

Here's to lots of laughter, lots of learning, and lots of just plain craziness!!! May your classroom or library be filled with all three.

—Tony Fredericks

ACKNOWLEDGMENTS

This book would not have been possible without the continued support and enthusiasm of many individuals. Most important, it was influenced, encouraged, and promoted by thousands of teachers and librarians throughout North America who so warmly embraced the original *Frantic Frogs and Other Frankly Fractured Folktales for Readers Theatre* (1993). Their sincere passion for the energy of readers theatre as a viable language arts activity was a powerful stimulant for the creation of this sequel. I am forever indebted to their zeal for integrating readers theatre throughout their instructional programs, as well as their zest for teaching with this most creative technique.

Once again, I am indebted to my daughter Rebecca, whose incredibly creative illustrations have graced another book. Her attention to detail, wondrous blending of line and shape, and equally imaginative interpretation of character and story have added immeasurably to this latest venture. As always, her artistic talent, wit, and charm have made this literary creation a far, far better publication.

To Little Miss Muffet, who throws one mean party with all that curds and whey and stuff. (By the way, did you ever find out what happened to the spider and her date, the fly?)

A note of sympathy to Chicken Little and that incident with the falling sky. I sure hope your new therapist helps you get to your "inner chicken."

To Jack and Jill and their endless trips to that darned well at the top of the hill. (Hey, have you guys ever thought about indoor plumbing?)

To the Ugly Duckling, who really made one middle-aged author feel really good (by comparison, that is) when he looked into the mirror.

To Little Red Riding Hood, who has to put up with all those hairy creatures lurking in the woods. Thanks so much for letting me spend the night at Granny's while I was interviewing the Three Little Pigs over in the other story.

To Robin Hood and his Merry Men and the great sing-along on Saturday night in the middle of the forest. You guys really know how to PARTY HEARTY!! (and that mead was pretty darned good, too)!

To Kermit and all his amphibious friends down at the swamp. I don't know how you guys do it, but I'm still amazed at your ability to snap those flies right out of the air. I mean, those are some wicked tongues!

To King Midas—you really touched me with all your generosity.

And, most important, to kids everywhere—whose silliness is the inspiration for these stories, whose craziness is the eternal elixir for one somewhat balding children's author, whose wackiness fills classrooms and libraries with ceaseless laughter, and whose enthusiasm makes teaching such a constant joy—goes my unwavering gratitude and admiration.

A VERY BRIEF NOTE TO ALL THE PURCHASERS (a.k.a. Highly Intelligent Individuals) OF THE FIRST *FRANTIC FROGS . . .* BOOK

O.K., you're back for another round of

- wildness,

- weirdness,

- wackiness,

- uncontrollable giggles and guffaws,

- truckloads of chuckles and chortles,

- a plethora of snickers and smirks,

- a caboodle (hey, it's a real word—look it up!) of howls and haw-haws,

- a classroom overflowing with mirth and merriment,

- a library brimming with cackling and cheering,

- a language arts program littered with hilarity and happiness,

- tomfoolery,

- badinage (another real word—no, really!),

- buffoonery,

- jollity,

- high glee,

- joy,

- jocundity, and

- joviality.

In other words, your sense of humor is just about as demented as mine and you wish nothing more than to inflict it (once again) on an innocent, unknowing, and unassuming group of very impressionable youngsters. You might as well admit it—helping kids see the humor and fun that can be had with stories, legends, and folktales is one of the most incredible experiences you're likely to inflict on any class. (I mean, besides that day when you came to school in your "Little Bo Peep" costume.)

Do you remember all the looniness and silly times you had when you shared the following readers theatre scripts (from the first *Frantic Frogs* book) with your students?

- "Don't Kiss Sleeping Beauty, She's Got Really Bad Breath"

- "Rapunzel Gets a Really Lousy Hairdo"

- "The Big Bad Wolf Goes to the Doctor to Find Out Why He Can't Huff and Puff Anymore"

- "Jack Climbs to the Top of a Very Tall Vegetable and Finds a Very Large Individual with an Attitude Problem"

Your classroom or library was undoubtedly awash in barrels of vivacity and reams of jocularity (hey, I'm not making these words up—they're all right here in my brand new *Webster's Collegiate Dictionary*).

And now you're back for more!

Well, you won't be disappointed. For here are dozens of new scripts, partial scripts, and really strange script titles that you can wreak on that unsuspecting gang of students in your charge. And, as before, they'll experience the insane joy that can come from wildly creative readers theatre adaptations of some of their favorite folktales, legends, and stories. Also, as before, you'll unleash an avalanche (or a mega-tsunami) of creative writing opportunities for your students. They will be unduly inspired and undeniably stimulated to create their own scripts with their own array of weird characters, wacky settings, and wild adventures. The result, as before, will be a language arts curriculum or library program that will be the envy of every other teacher in the school and/or district (although some administrators may have a few things to say about you—but let's not worry about them just yet).

So, welcome back!

Now, let's party!!

P.S. Oh, in case you were wondering why it took me soooooooooo long to come up with a sequel to the first *Frantic Frogs* book (published in 1993), let's just say that I had a very, V-E-R-Y, VERY long "honey-do" list!

Part I

A BUNCH OF EDUCATIONAL STUFF YOU GOTTA KNOW BEFORE YOU READ ALL THE REALLY WEIRD STUFF IN THE REST OF THIS BOOK
(a.k.a. the Introduction)

"ONCE UPON A TIME . . ."

Say the words "Once upon a time . . ." to any adult and you will probably see a smile slip across his or her face. Those are magical words—words that conjure up legends, fairy tales, and stories of long ago. For most of us, they bring back pleasant memories of someone (our parents or a favorite teacher) reading (aloud) a story or book. Those words may remind us of simpler times—times long before we had to worry about home mortgages, saving for our kids' college tuition, retirement plans, or even behavioral objectives. The memories were sweet and the recollections were always pleasurable.

Think how those same four words might impact the students with whom you work. Think of the mental journeys or creative adventures you can share with youngsters as you lead them through the magical world of children's literature. Imaginations are stimulated and minds are filled with the delicious sounds of language in action! It is that language—the language of feeling, emotion, and passion—that excites youngsters and helps them appreciate the role literature and books play in their everyday lives (as they have for generations).

And what better way to bring children's literature alive than through the magic of readers theatre. Readers theatre offers youngsters interesting and unique insights into the utility of language and its value in both its printed and oral forms. It is "language arts" in its purest form; it is literature brought to life.

WHAT IS READERS THEATRE?

Readers theatre is a storytelling device that stimulates the imagination and promotes all of the language arts. Simply stated, it is an oral interpretation of a piece of literature, read in a dramatic style. Readers theatre is an act of involvement, an opportunity to share, a time to creatively interact with others, and a personal interpretation of what can be or could be. Readers theatre provides numerous opportunities for youngsters to make stories and literature come alive and pulsate with their own unique brand of perception and vision. In so doing, literature becomes personal and reflective—children have a breadth of opportunities to be authentic users of language.

The magic of storytelling has been a tradition of every culture and civilization since the dawn of language. It binds human beings and celebrates their heritage as no other language art can. It is part and parcel of the human experience, because it underscores the values and experiences we cherish as well as those we seek to share with each other. Nowhere is this more important than in today's classroom or library. Perhaps it is a natural part of who we are—that stories command our attention and help us appreciate the values, ideas, and traditions we hold dear. So, too, should students have those same experiences and those same pleasures.

Storytelling conjures up all sorts of visions and possibilities—faraway lands; magnificent adventures; enchanted princes; beautiful princesses; evil wizards and wicked witches; a few dragons and demons; a couple of castles and cottages; perhaps a mysterious forest or two; and certainly tales of mystery, intrigue, and adventure.

These are stories of tradition and timelessness, tales that enchant, mystify, and excite through a marvelous weaving of characters, settings, and plots . . . tales that have stood the test of time. Our senses are stimulated, our mental images are energized, and our experiences are fortified through the magic of storytelling.

Storytelling is also a way of sharing the power and intrigue of language. I suppose part of my belief that storytelling is the quintessential classroom activity lies in the fact that it is an opportunity to bring life, vitality, and substance to the two-dimensional letters and words on a printed page. It is also an interpersonal activity—a "never-fail" way to connect with minds and souls and hearts.

When children are provided with regular opportunities to become storytellers, they develop a personal stake in the literature shared. They also begin to cultivate personal interpretations of that literature—interpretations that lead to higher levels of appreciation and comprehension. Practicing and performing stories is an involvement endeavor—one that demonstrates and utilizes numerous languaging activities.

READERS THEATRE AND FLUENCY

Readers theatre is an instructional method that enhances reading fluency. Reading researchers have identified five primary areas of reading instruction for all readers: (1) phonemic awareness, (2) phonics, (3) fluency, (4) vocabulary, and (5) comprehension. When teachers and librarians incorporate readers theatre into their respective programs, youngsters are offered multiple opportunities to understand the natural rhythm and flow of language.

Fluency is the ability to read text accurately and quickly. It's reading in which words are recognized automatically. When fluent readers read, they group words quickly to help them gain meaning from what the material. Their oral reading sounds natural, and their silent reading is smooth and unencumbered by an overemphasis on word-by-word analysis. Fluent readers are those who do not need to concentrate on the decoding of words; rather, they can direct their attention to their comprehension of text. In short, fluent readers are able to recognize words and comprehend at the same time. They are able to make connections between their background knowledge and ideas in a book or other piece of writing. I often like to think of fluency as the essential stepping stone between phonetic ability and comprehension.

It's important to remember that fluency is something that develops over time. Fluency instruction must be integrated into all aspects of the reading program as the "bridge" that students need to be successful comprehenders. Fluency is not an isolated element of the reading curriculum; rather, it is an essential component that models and provides active involvement opportunities for students as they transition from decoding to comprehension. A recent study by the National Assessment of Educational Progress (NAEP) found a direct correlation between fluency and reading comprehension. In fact, students who score low on measures of fluency also score low on measures of comprehension. The implication is that efforts designed to foster fluency development will have a direct impact on students' growth and development in comprehension development.

Not surprisingly, one of the most effective ways teachers and librarians can promote fluency development is through the use of readers theatre. Its advantages are twofold:

- It offers positive models of fluent reading as demonstrated by a teacher or other accomplished readers.

- It provides readers with a legitimate reason for rereading text in an enjoyable and engaging format.

Students should practice fluency in authentic texts and in authentic situations. Reading will be portrayed as a pleasurable activity, with both purpose and interest. As students take on the roles of characters (in readers theatre, for example), they also take on the roles of competent readers.

WHAT IS THE VALUE OF READERS THEATRE?

Here's what I like so much about readers theatre: It encourages students to interpret literature without the constraints of skills, memorization, or evaluation. Readers theatre allows children to breathe life and substance into literature—an interpretation that is neither right nor wrong, since it will be colored by kids' unique perspectives, experiences, and vision. The readers' interpretation of a piece of literature is intrinsically more valuable than some predetermined "translation" that might be found in a teacher's manual, for example.

Here are some of the many values I see in readers theatre:

- Children can learn about the major features of children's literature—plot, theme, setting, point of view, and characterization. This occurs when they are provided with opportunities to design and construct their own readers theatre scripts (after experiencing prepared scripts such as those in this book).

- Readers theatre helps students focus on the integration of all the language arts—reading, writing, speaking, and listening. Children begin to see that effective communication and the comprehension of text are inexorably intertwined.

- Readers theatre supports a holistic philosophy of instruction and allows children to become responsible learners—those who seek answers to their own self-initiated inquiries.

- Readers theatre is informal and relaxed. It does not require elaborate props, scenery, or costumes. It can be set up in any classroom or library. It does not require large sums of money to "make it happen." And it can be "put on" in any kind of environment—formal or informal.

- Teachers and librarians have also discovered that readers theatre is an excellent way to enhance the development of important communication skills. Voice projection, intonation, inflection, and pronunciation skills are all promoted through any readers theatre production.

- Creative and critical thinking are enhanced through the utilization of readers theatre. Children are active participants in the interpretation and delivery of a story; they develop thinking skills that are divergent rather than convergent.

- Readers theatre allows children to experience stories in a supportive and nonthreatening format that underscores their active involvement.

- Readers theatre stimulates the imagination and the creation of visual images. It has been substantiated that when youngsters are provided with opportunities to create their own mental images, their comprehension and appreciation of a piece of writing will be enhanced considerably.

- Readers theatre offers positive models of fluent reading and provides readers with a legitimate reason for rereading text in an enjoyable and engaging format.

- The development and enhancement of self-concept is facilitated through readers theatre. Since children are working in concert with other children in a supportive atmosphere, their self-esteem mushrooms accordingly.

- Readers theatre is a participatory event. The characters as well as the audience are all intimately involved in the design, structure, and delivery of the story. As such, children begin to realize that reading is not a solitary activity, but one that can be shared and discussed with others.

- Since it is the performance that drives readers theatre, children are given more opportunities to invest themselves and their personalities in the production of a readers theatre. The same story may be subject to several different presentations, depending on the group or the individual youngsters involved.

- When children are provided with opportunities to write and/or script their own readers theatre, their writing abilities are supported and encouraged. As children become familiar with the design and format of readers theatre scripts, they can begin to utilize their own creative talents in designing their own scripts.

- Readers theatre is valuable for non-English-speaking children (ELL or ESL learners). It provides them with positive models of language usage and interpretation. It allows them to see "language in action" and the various ways in which language can be used.

- Readers theatre enhances the development of cooperative learning strategies. It requires youngsters to work together toward a common goal and supports their efforts in doing so.

- Readers theatre is fun! Children of all ages have delighted in using readers theatre for many years. It is delightful and stimulating, encouraging and fascinating, relevant and personal. It is a classroom or library activity filled with a cornucopia of possibilities and promises.

HOW TO PRESENT READERS THEATRE

It is important to remember that there is no single way to present readers theatre. What follows are some ideas you and the youngsters with whom you work may wish to keep in mind as you put on the productions in this book—whether in a classroom setting or the school library.

Preparing Scripts

One of the advantages of using readers theatre in the classroom or library is the lack of extra work or preparation time necessary to get "up and running." By using the scripts in this book, your preparation time is minimal.

- After a script has been selected for presentation, make sufficient copies. A copy of the script should be provided for each actor. In addition, two or three extra copies (one for you and "replacement" copies for scripts that are accidentally damaged or lost) are also a good idea. Copies for the audience are unnecessary and are not suggested.

- Each script can be bound between two sheets of colored construction paper or poster board. Bound scripts tend to formalize the presentation a little and lend an air of professionalism to the actors.

- Highlight each character's speaking parts with different color highlighter pens. This helps youngsters track their parts without being distracted by the dialogue of others.

Starting Out

Introducing the concept of readers theatre to students for the first time may be as simple as sharing a script with an entire class and "walking" youngsters through the design and delivery of that script.

- Emphasize that a readers theatre performance does not require any memorization of the script. It's the interpretation and performance that count.

- You may wish to read through an entire script aloud, taking on the various roles. Let students know how easy and comfortable this process is.

- Encourage selected volunteers to read assigned parts of a sample script to the entire class. Readers should stand or sit in a circle so that other classmates can observe them.

- Provide opportunities for additional re-readings using other volunteers. Plan time to discuss the ease of presentation and the different interpretations offered by different readers.

- Readers should have an opportunity to practice their scripts before presenting them to an audience. Take some time to discuss voice intonation, facial gestures, body movements, and other features that could be used to enhance the presentation.

- Allow children the opportunity to suggest their own modifications, adaptations, or interpretations of the script. They will undoubtedly be "in tune" with the interests and perceptions of their peers and can offer some distinctive and personal interpretations.

- Encourage students to select nonstereotypical roles in any readers theatre script. For example, boys can take on female roles and girls can take on male roles; the smallest person in the class can take on the role of a giant, fire-breathing dragon (for example); or a shy student can take on the role of a boastful, bragging giant. Provide sufficient opportunities for students to expand and extend their appreciation of readers theatre through a variety of "out of character" roles.

Staging

Staging involves the physical location of the readers as well as any necessary movements. Unlike in a more formal play, the movements are often minimal. The emphasis is more on presentation and less on action.

- For most presentations readers will stand or sit on stools or chairs. The physical location of each reader has been indicated for each of the scripts in this book.

- If there are many characters in the presentation, it may be advantageous to have characters in the rear (upstage) standing while those in the front (downstage) are placed on stools or chairs. This ensures that the audience will both see and hear each actor.

- Usually all the characters will be on stage throughout the duration of the presentation. For most presentations it is not necessary to have characters enter and exit. If you place the characters on stools, they can face the audience when they are involved in a particular scene and then turn around whenever they are not involved in a scene.

- You may wish to make simple, hand-lettered signs with the name of each character. Loop a piece of string or yarn through each sign and hang it around the neck of each respective character. This will allow the audience to see the identity of each character throughout the presentation.

- Each reader will have her or his own copy of the script in a paper cover (see above). If possible, use a music stand for each reader's script (this allows readers to use their hands for dramatic interpretations as necessary).

- Several presentations have a narrator to set up the story. The narrator serves to establish the place and time of the story for the audience so that the characters can "jump into" their parts from the beginning of the story. Typically, the narrator is separated from the other "actors" and can be identified by a simple sign.

Props

Two of the positive features of readers theatre are its ease of preparation and its ease of presentation. Informality is a hallmark of any readers theatre script.

- Much of the setting for a story should take place in the audience's mind. Elaborate scenery is not necessary—simple props are often the best. For example:
  - A branch or potted plant can serve as a tree.
  - A drawing on the chalkboard can illustrate a building.
  - A hand-lettered sign can designate one part of the staging area as a particular scene (e.g., swamp, castle, field, forest).
  - Children's toys can be used for uncomplicated props (e.g., telephone, vehicles).
  - A sheet of aluminum foil or a remnant of blue cloth can be used to simulate a lake or pond.

- Costumes for the actors are unnecessary. A few simple items may be suggested by students. For example:
  - Hats, scarves, or aprons can be used by major characters.
  - A paper cutout can serve as a tie, button, or badge.
  - Old clothing (borrowed from parents) can be used as warranted.

- Some teachers and librarians have discovered that the addition of appropriate background music or sound effects can enhance a readers theatre presentation.

- It's important to remember that the emphasis in readers theatre is on the reading—not on any accompanying "features." The best presentations are often the simplest.

Delivery

I've often found it advantageous to let students know that the only difference between a readers theatre presentation and a movie role is the fact that they will have a script in their hands. This allows them to focus more on *presenting* a script rather than *memorizing* a script.

- When first introduced to readers theatre, students often have a tendency to "read into" their scripts. Encourage students to look up from their scripts and interact with other characters or the audience as necessary

- Practicing the script beforehand can eliminate the problem of students burying their heads in the pages. Children will come to understand the need to involve the audience as much as possible in the development of the story.

- Voice projection and delivery are important in allowing the audience to understand character actions. The proper mood and intent need to be established—possible when children are familiar and comfortable with each character's "style."

- Again, the emphasis is on delivery, so be sure to suggest different types of voice (i.e., angry, irritated, calm, frustrated, excited, etc.) that children may wish to use for their particular character(s).

Post-Presentation

As a wise author once said, "The play's the thing." So it is with readers theatre. In other words, the mere act of presenting a readers theatre script is complete in and of itself. It is not necessary, or even required, to do any type of formalized evaluation after readers theatre. Once again, the emphasis is on informality. Readers theatre should and can be a pleasurable and stimulating experience for children.

What follows are a few ideas you may want to share with students. In doing so, you will be providing youngsters with important learning opportunities that extend and promote all aspects of your reading and language arts program.

- After a presentation, discuss with students how the script enhanced or altered the original story.

- Invite students to suggest other characters who could be added to the script.

- Invite students to suggest new or alternate dialogue for various characters

- Invite students to suggest new or different setting(s) for the script.

- Invite students to talk about their reactions to various characters' expressions, tone of voice, presentations, or dialogues.

- After a presentation, invite youngsters to suggest any modifications or changes they think could be used with the script.

Presenting a readers theatre script need not be an elaborate or extensive production. As children become more familiar with and polished in using readers theatre, they will be able to suggest a multitude of presentation possibilities for future scripts. It is important to help children assume a measure of self-initiated responsibility in the delivery of any readers theatre. In so doing, you will be helping to ensure their personal engagement and active participation in this most valuable of language arts activities.

HOW TO CREATE YOUR OWN READERS THEATRE

It is hoped that you and your students will find an abundance of readers theatre scripts in this book for use in your own classroom or library. But these scripts should also serve as an impetus for the creation of your own scripts. By providing opportunities for children to begin designing their own readers theatre scripts, you will be offering them an exciting new arena for the utilization and enhancement of their writing abilities.

Following are some suggestions you and your students may wish to consider in developing your own readers theatre scripts. They are purposely generic in nature and can be used with almost all kinds of reading material. Of course the emphasis in this book is on humorous readers theatre scripts—particularly those dealing with fairy tales, Mother Goose rhymes, fables, legends, and other children's classics; these ideas will help children create their own fractured fairy tales as part of their process writing program.

Select an Appropriate Story

Humor works best when it touches on something with which we are familiar. For this reason, the stories selected for this book have come from the experiential background of most children—Mother Goose, legends, tall tales, fairy tales, and the like—and then expanded (far) beyond their original design. The stories children select for the development of their own readers theatre scripts should also be familiar ones. They will be able to build on that familiarity for a humorous effect.

I have found that most, if not all, fairy tales and Mother Goose rhymes can be adapted to a readers theatre format; it just depends on how twisted one's sense of humor is. That said, the best stories to use are those with tight plots and clear endings, distinctive characters, engaging dialogue, and universal themes (e.g., good over evil, love conquers all, logic is more powerful than strength).

In selecting stories, the number of characters is important. I have found that two to six characters work best. For that reason, some minor characters may be eliminated and their dialogue "absorbed" by other characters. On the other hand, one or two brand new characters may have to be developed to facilitate the pace of the story. It is important that the staging area not be crowded with too many characters, distracting the audience's attention.

Illustrate and Model

Initially, children may be unfamiliar with the format of readers theatre (although after experiencing several of the scripts in this book, they will be quite used to the design). It is important to discuss with children that readers theatre is very similar to movie and television scripts and written in much the same way. As in Hollywood, the intent is to take a basic story and turn it into a play or movie. With your children, discuss the original stories used as the foundation of these scripts and the resultant readers theatre design(s).

Invite students to model the steps used in designing a readers theatre script. I have found it advantageous to use a sheet of chart pack paper, a large piece of poster board, or the overhead projector. Using a familiar story, I begin to rewrite it so that the entire group can see the steps I use. These steps might include

- rewriting the title to give it a more humorous slant;

- eliminating unnecessary dialogue or minor characters;

- inserting a narrator at strategic points to advance the action or identify specific scenes;

- adding words that describe the tone of voice used by a specific character (e.g., "rapidly," "irritated," "confused") ;

- underlining or boldfacing the names of characters for easy identification;

- creating new dialogue, characters, or settings to advance the story or produce a humorous situation; and

- consideration of the props necessary for the story.

It should be pointed out that there is no ideal series of steps to follow in the design of readers theatre scripts. It is important, however, that children have some models to follow so that they will be encouraged and supported in the creation of their own scripts.

Adapting the Story

After children have experienced the scripts in this book, they will be familiar with ways in which a fairy tale or legend can be turned into a humorous readers theatre script. When you allow children opportunities to develop their own humorous scripts, you will soon discover a wonderfully creative spirit permeating all aspects of your language arts program.

Obviously, humor comes in many forms. Some methods you and your students may wish to consider in transforming familiar tales into wild and wacky ones are discussed below.

Exaggeration: Blow something completely out of proportion. Instead of "Little Boy Blue," a story title could be "Just Another Tale About Some Kid Who Dresses Up in Blue and Sleeps in Haystacks." In place of "Humpty Dumpty," the story title could be "This Very Round Fellow Who Sits on Top of a Wall All Day Long." Exaggeration can include story titles and extend to character personalities and physical descriptions as well as story settings.

Colloquialisms: Allow children to use language and idioms with which they are most familiar (some mild censorship may be necessary). Slang terms and phrases in the mouths of familiar characters can be quite funny. For example, Simple Simon could say, "Hey, dude, would you like to have some 'Ding Dongs' instead of pie?" Or one of the Three Blind Mice could say, "Hey, stop buggin' us. We've had it up to here with that woman chasing us with a knife." Obviously, a selective use of colloquialisms is preferable to a script rife with slang.

Reversals: Change characters' personalities so that they are completely different. For example, instead of the typical evil stepmother, children can create a really nice stepmother; instead of an enchanted prince, have children develop a fairly stupid prince; instead of a fire-breathing dragon, have children create a shy reptile trying to kick the smoking habit. Reversals (or partial reversals) can be used for the setting of a story, too. Instead of a gingerbread house, have children design a condo in the suburbs; instead of a farmhouse, have children use a beach hut in Hawaii; instead of a deep dark forest, have children set a story in a shopping mall.

Anachronisms: Use an object that is totally out of place in the story. For example, instead of the wicked witch traveling on a broomstick, she can use her frequent flyer miles on an airplane; instead of characters traveling by horse and carriage from one castle to another, they can call each other with their cell phones; instead of sending a poison pen letter by messenger, it can be faxed.

Misdirection: Misdirection is when the reader or listener is misled about to the outcome of a story. For example, the story of Old Mother Hubbard can be told;, except the new ending has the dog looking for food for the old woman. Or Little Miss Muffet could order French fried spiders at her local fast food restaurant instead of slurping curds and whey.

Character changes: Give familiar characters entirely new personalities or whole new physical features. For example, Humpty Dumpty gives up his day job and goes to work as a short order cook at McDonalds. The fire-breathing dragon gets a loan from the bank and markets his own brand of barbecue sauce. The old woman in the shoe branches out and builds a condo complex of sneakers and pumps. The troll goes to charm school and learns to eat with a knife and fork.

Combination formula: In a combination formula the writer combines two very different subjects or elements into an entirely new arrangement. For example, the eating habits of a frog can be combined with the eating habits of a prince to create a prince who sits around the castle all day snatching flies out of the air with his three-foot tongue. The personality of a mouse can be combined with the personality of a real estate developer to create a small rodent who sells nests to families of rats. The features of a fairy tale cottage can be combined with the features of a suburban housing development to create a development of condos for wicked witches only (sorry, no young children allowed).

Preparation and Writing

Children should be encouraged to work together to design their readers theatre scripts. Small groups of four to five children will allow for a multiplicity of options and suggestions for scripting a familiar story. It would be advantageous to appoint one youngster within each group to serve as the "scribe" or "recorder." Each recorder should understand that writing goes through many stages, so the first couple of ideas are just that—initial ones, which can be eliminated or expanded according to the wishes and desires of the group.

Have each group's recorder write the names of all the identified characters down the left side of a large sheet of poster paper. Other members of a group can suggest possible dialogue for each of the characters as well as the narrator. Movements and actions can also be suggested by group members. I have found it advantageous to consider any props, stage directions, and "set up" after the initial draft of the script. In this way, children can concentrate on the creative expression of their ideas without worrying about some of the minor aspects of their script—all of which can be added later.

Production and Practice

Provide student groups with opportunities to "try out" their drafts on other groups of children. They should watch for the flow of the story, the pace, appropriate dialogue, and, of course, the humor of their script. Just as a playwright will go through many drafts of a play, so, too, should children realize that they may also need time to work out the kinks in their productions. By trying out their various drafts on other children, they will have an opportunity to structure and restructure their readers theatre script for maximum impact.

THE YOUNG AND ALLURING PRINCESS (A.K.A. A BRIGHT AND CLEVER SCHOOL LIBRARIAN) AND READERS THEATRE

What both elementary teachers and school librarians have long known intuitively, and what has been validated with a significant body of research, is that the literature shared in both classroom and library has wide-ranging and long-lasting implications for the educational and social development of children. More important, however, is the unassailable fact that when teachers and librarians join together to promote literature collaboratively, they are opening incredible windows that expand the influence of that literature and extend the learning opportunities for youngsters as never before.

In preparation for writing this book, I talked with school librarians and teachers throughout the United States. I discovered that the "collaboration factor" had a significant influence on the ultimate success of readers theatre. A substantial level of cooperation between the classroom teacher and the school librarian was essential if readers theatre was to be made a successful element and a dynamic feature of any language arts curriculum. The partnership between teacher and librarian was, and continues to be, the crucial element in the success children enjoy within and throughout any academic endeavor.

But as you might imagine, this partnership does not happen overnight. It involves a mutual sharing of ideas, possibilities, and projects. But when teachers and librarians band together, the curricular effect of readers theatre can be expanded exponentially. It involves trust and coordination, but the overall effect is more than worth the effort.

Benefits

In my discussions with elementary school librarians and classroom teachers, I discovered the following benefits in a collaborative partnership between these two individuals:

- Readers theatre projects can be designed, developed, and taught over an extended period of time (days, weeks).

- The Reading/English Language Arts Standards can be promoted in a coordinated and systematic fashion.

- Library programs can be effectively coordinated with classroom programs for both the short and long term.

- More time is available for instructional purposes. A partnership between a teacher and the school librarian can expand the instructional possibilities of readers theatre.

- Language arts is promoted as a continuous activity rather than a subject taught only in a classroom.

- There is a greater emphasis on language arts as a continuous process of problem solving and critical thinking.

- Language arts can be woven into all aspects of the elementary curriculum. Readers theatre offers instructional possibilities that expand and extend teaching and learning opportunities beyond traditional practices.

- Both literature and readers theatre are promoted as viable and exciting models of literacy in action.

- Cooperative teaching and cooperative learning can be promoted simultaneously.

Forging the Partnership

When teachers and librarians work together, great things happen. When they do so as an essential ingredient of the reading/language arts curriculum, then fantastic things happen! Following is a listing of the ways in which teachers and librarians can develop a partnership that is mutually supportive, educationally sound, and dynamically oriented toward a coordinated approach to readers theatre.

- Teachers and librarians should plan to team teach readers theatre units.

- Teachers should invite the librarian into their classrooms to introduce readers theatre and any accompanying literature.

- Librarians should invite teachers into the library to introduce readers theatre (to their classes) and any accompanying literature.

- Teachers should provide the school librarian with a list of language arts topics and assignments to be tackled throughout the year. Teachers should then work with the librarian to make suggestions regarding available resources—specifically readers theatre.

- Teachers and librarians should develop joint projects in which selected literature is introduced in the library and followed up with specific instructional activities (i.e., readers theatre) in the classroom.

- Teachers and librarians should develop joint projects in which selected literature is introduced into the classroom and followed up with specific instructional activities (i.e., readers theatre) in the library.

- Librarians should introduce students to specific literature selections, with appropriate follow-up activities (i.e., readers theatre) for use in the classroom.

- Teachers should introduce students to specific literature selections, with appropriate follow-up activities (i.e., readers theatre) for use in the library.

- Invite students to create their own readers theatre scripts (see part IV and appendix B) after reading selected (and assigned) books in the library.

The possibilities for a coordinated approach to readers theatre—between school librarians and classroom teachers—are astronomical! Students are provided with engaging and lasting learning opportunities, teachers have multiple ways of sharing the vitality of language arts, and librarians can promote literature far beyond the walls of the school library. When teachers and librarians work together, the educational benefits of readers theatre mushroom exponentially.

STANDARDS, SCHMANDARDS (WHAT THE GUYS IN THE DEPARTMENT OF ED. WANT)

In response to a demand for a cohesive set of standards that address overall curriculum design and comprehensive student performance expectations in reading and language arts education, the International Reading Association, in concert with the National Council of Teachers of English, developed and promulgated the IRA/NCTE *Standards for the English Language Arts.* These standards provide a focused outline of the essential components of a well-structured language arts curriculum.

The 12 standards place an emphasis on literacy development as a lifelong process—one that starts well before youngsters enter school and continues throughout their lifetimes. Thus, these standards are intentionally integrative and multidisciplinary. Just as important, they support and underscore the values of readers theatre (see above) as a multipurpose language arts activity—one appropriate for both classroom and library.

The chart on page 17 provides an abridged version of the *Standards.* Along with each standard (as appropriate) is how readers theatre serves as a valuable and innovative teaching tool in support of those standards.

English/Language Arts Standards*	Readers Theatre Support
1. Students are engaged with a wide variety of print and nonprint resources.	Readers theatre introduces students to a wealth of literature from a variety of literary sources.
2. Students are exposed to many genres of literature.	Readers theatre offers students a range of reading materials that span the eight basic genres of children's literature.
3. Students use many reading strategies to comprehend text.	Readers theatre invites students to assume an active role in comprehension development through their engagement and participation.
4. Students communicate in a variety of ways.	Readers theatre invites students to practice reading, writing, listening, and speaking in an enjoyable and educative process.
5. Students learn through writing.	Readers theatre encourages students to develop their own scripts and share them with a receptive audience.
6. Students use a variety of language conventions to understand text.	Readers theatre encourages students to discuss and understand how language conveys ideas.
7. Students are involved in personally meaningful research projects.	Readers theatre invites youngsters to examine and explore stories from a wide range of perspectives.
8. Students are comfortable with technology.	
9. Students gain an appreciation of language in a variety of venues.	Readers theatre encourages students to look at language and language use in a host of educational formats.
10. Non-English-speaking students develop competencies in all the language arts.	Readers theatre offers models of English use in a fun and engaging format.
11. Students are members of a host of literacy communities.	Readers theatre provides creative, investigative, and dynamic opportunities to see language in action.
12. Students use language for personal reasons.	Readers theatre offers innumerable opportunities for students to engage in personally enriching language activities.

*Modified and abridged from *Standards for the English Language Arts*, International Reading Association/National Council of Teachers of English, 1996.

When reviewing the standards above, it should become evident that many elements of those standards can be promoted through the regular and systematic introduction of readers theatre into the elementary language arts curriculum. Equally important is the fact that those standards assist teachers and librarians in validating the impact and significance of readers theatre as a viable and valuable instructional tool—in language arts and throughout the entire elementary curriculum.

REFERENCES

Fredericks, Anthony D. *African Legends, Myths, and Folktales for Readers Theatre.* Westport, CT: Teacher Ideas Press, 2008.

———. *Frantic Frogs and Other Frankly Fractured Folktales for Readers Theatre.* Westport, CT: Teacher Ideas Press, 1993.

———. *Mother Goose Readers Theatre for Beginning Readers.* Westport, CT: Teacher Ideas Press, 2007.

———. *Nonfiction Readers Theatre for Beginning Readers.* Westport, CT: Teacher Ideas Press, 2007.

———. *Readers Theatre for American History.* Westport, CT: Teacher Ideas Press, 2001.

———. *Science Fiction Readers Theatre.* Westport, CT: Teacher Ideas Press, 2002.

———. *Silly Salamanders and Other Slightly Stupid Stories for Readers Theatre.* Westport, CT: Teacher Ideas Press, 2000.

———. *Songs and Rhymes Readers Theatre for Beginning Readers.* Westport, CT: Teacher Ideas Press, 2007.

———. *Tadpole Tales and Other Totally Terrific Treats for Readers Theatre.* Westport, CT: Teacher Ideas Press, 1997.

Part II

ARE YOU READY?: HERE'S ALL THE REALLY WILD AND WACKY SCRIPTS THAT YOU'VE BEEN WAITING FOR

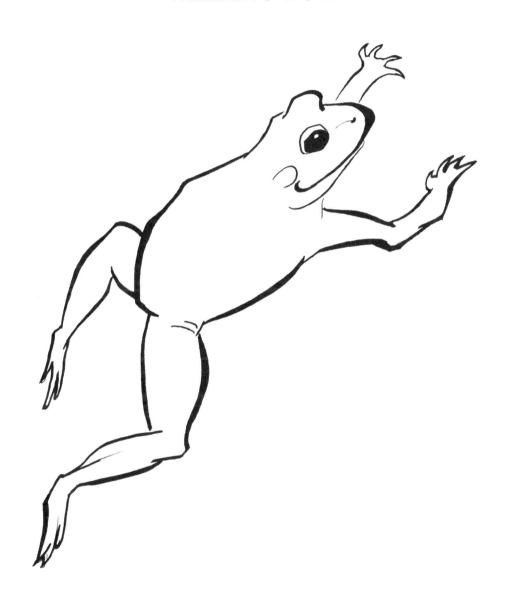

ONCE UPON A TIME IN "ONCE UPON A TIME" TIME

STAGING:

The narrator sits on a tall stool to the side of the staging area. The other characters can be standing or sitting on stools.

```
      Really Strange Author              Intelligent Student
              X                                  X
              Really Cool Teacher              Very Bright Student
                      X                              X
  Narrator
      X
```

NARRATOR:	[very serious] The story you are about to see is true. Only the names have been changed to protect the innocent.
REALLY STRANGE AUTHOR:	Hey, I'm really strange and unusual.
INTELLIGENT STUDENT:	Yes, we know that!
REALLY STRANGE AUTHOR:	How do you know that?
REALLY COOL TEACHER:	Well, all authors are strange and unusual.
REALLY STRANGE AUTHOR:	[confused] Oh, I didn't know that!
REALLY COOL TEACHER:	Well, some authors are stranger and more unusual than others. We know that because we read lots of stories in this class. We share fairy tales and legends and adventure stories and biographies and science fiction and nonfiction and lots of other stuff from all kinds of authors.
VERY BRIGHT STUDENT:	Yeah, it's really neat. We get to listen to stories from many different genres and from many different parts of the world.
INTELLIGENT STUDENT:	We also get to read and listen to all kinds of different authors, too. We get to study the lives of some of our favorite authors and examine some of the books they've written.

From *MORE Frantic Frogs and Other Frankly Fractured Folktales for Readers Theatre* by Anthony D. Fredericks. Westport, CT: Teacher Ideas Press. Copyright © 2008.

NARRATOR:	Why don't you tell the Really Strange Author some of the things you do with those stories?
INTELLIGENT STUDENT:	Okay. We also get to do some readers theatre plays.
REALLY STRANGE AUTHOR:	Readers theatre? What's that?
VERY BRIGHT STUDENT:	That's when we assign speaking parts for various characters in a story and then we get to read the story out loud in the roles of those characters.
REALLY COOL TEACHER:	Yes, it has been discovered that readers theatre helps students gain an appreciation for literature because they help make that literature, or stories, come alive through their own personal interpretations.
REALLY STRANGE AUTHOR:	Okay, let me get this straight. You [points to Really Cool Teacher] give students some stories that they will read aloud to the other kids in the classroom.
REALLY COOL TEACHER:	That's right. Those stories are actually like movie scripts. They have speaking parts for each of several characters and the students read them aloud. They don't have to memorize their parts. But they can act them out just like real actors in a real play.
REALLY STRANGE AUTHOR:	Hey, that sounds like it could be a lot of fun.
VERY BRIGHT STUDENT:	It is! We learn a lot about how stories are constructed . . . .
INTELLIGENT STUDENT:	And we learn about the elements of a good story like plot and theme and point of view and characterization and setting . . . .
REALLY COOL TEACHER:	And it helps students improve their fluency—or the smooth reading of a story.
VERY BRIGHT STUDENT:	Don't forget the other thing.
REALLY COOL TEACHER:	It also helps students improve their comprehension or understanding of stories.
REALLY STRANGE AUTHOR:	Hey, this readers theatre stuff sounds like it could be lots of fun along with lots of learning!

REALLY COOL TEACHER:	It is! And the best part is that all the work has been done for us.
REALLY STRANGE AUTHOR:	What do you mean?
REALLY COOL TEACHER:	Well, there are authors who write books of readers theatre scripts. Those books have lots of readers theatre scripts for a classroom or library along with ideas on how students can begin to create their own readers theatre scripts.
REALLY STRANGE AUTHOR:	Wow, those readers theatre authors sound like they are really the coolest of the cool! I bet they make a ton of money and are very handsome, too.
NARRATOR:	[aside to the audience] Obviously, this Really Strange Author person [points to Really Strange Author] hasn't been around for a while. I guess he or she doesn't know that authors don't make a ton of money, and they certainly aren't beautiful or handsome. They're just weird.
REALLY STRANGE AUTHOR:	Hey, I heard that! So, what you're saying is that I don't have to be rich or handsome to be a readers theatre author?
VERY BRIGHT STUDENT:	Nope. You just have to have lots of or really unusual and really weird ideas floating around in your head.
INTELLIGENT STUDENT:	And then you just put those really weird ideas into lots of scripts and collect them all into a book for teachers and librarians and students to use in the classroom.
REALLY COOL TEACHER:	But the best part comes when teachers and librarians and students get to share those readers theatre plays together. There are lots of giggles, lots of laughter, and lots of fun for everyone!
REALLY STRANGE AUTHOR:	Wow, that sounds great! What do I do now?
VERY BRIGHT STUDENT:	We suggest that you listen to some of the scripts we're going to do in this classroom.
INTELLIGENT STUDENT:	All the readers theatre scripts that we will be doing were written by a really strange and weird author . . . .

NARRATOR: [aside to audience] I think we should underline the words "strange" and "weird."

INTELLIGENT STUDENT: Anyway, a really strange and weird author, who has written a whole bunch of readers theatre books, wrote the scripts that we will perform in this classroom.

VERY BRIGHT STUDENT: And if you watch closely, you'll see how all of us get so much smarter and so much brighter and so much more intelligent than those kids in the other classes that don't use readers theatre.

INTELLIGENT STUDENT: And if you look carefully you'll notice that our teacher is known as the "Really Cool Teacher" [points to Really Cool Teacher] 'cause she uses lots of readers theatre scripts throughout the year.

REALLY STRANGE AUTHOR: Okay, I can't wait. Let's get started.

NARRATOR: And so it was that the Really Strange Author watched the class perform all sorts of readers theatre scripts. The classroom was filled with lots of learning and lots of laughter, just as he had been told it would be. He was amazed and delighted and thrilled beyond belief. Soon after, he went home and began writing a whole bunch of readers theatre scripts. And he became handsome and rich and lived happily ever after in a castle with a beautiful enchanted princess. The end!

LITTLE RED RIDING HOOD PUNCHES THE WOLF CHARACTER RIGHT IN THE KISSER

STAGING:

The characters can all be seated on tall stools. The narrator can be standing or seated on a stool on the edge of the staging area.

Cinderella	Snow White	Sleeping Beauty	Little Red Riding Hood	
X	X	X	X	
				Narrator
				X

NARRATOR:	Once upon a time a bunch of storybook characters got together for their monthly literary meeting, where they would talk about all the good literature (and some bad literature, too) that was being shared with students in schools all over the country. Well, as often happened, the discussion soon turned to some of the characters our friends here [points] have to deal with every time a story is read aloud.
LITTLE RED RIDING HOOD:	[upset] Hey, girls, you know what? I'm getting just a little sick and tired of always packing a little picnic basket full of goodies, skipping through the deep dark woods, and meeting this hairball of a character—whom the writers call a wolf—and then racing him over to Granny's house to see who can get to Granny's bed first.
SLEEPING BEAUTY:	*Zzzzzzzzzzzzz.*
SNOW WHITE:	Yeah, you got it tough, sister. Every time some teacher tells that story to her little students, you really get the "short end of the stick," so to speak. I mean, why does your adventure have to have some guy with an attitude problem, and who hasn't shaved in a month or more?
CINDERELLA:	Yeah, who do those writers think they are? How come we females always have to deal with mean, old, or ugly characters all the time? Just look in the library

From *MORE Frantic Frogs and Other Frankly Fractured Folktales for Readers Theatre* by Anthony D. Fredericks. Westport, CT: Teacher Ideas Press. Copyright © 2008.

and you'll see what I mean. How many stories do you know that are filled with handsome, polite, and very rich princes? Noooooooo, they're all filled with mean, old, or ugly dudes.

SLEEPING BEAUTY: *Zzzzzzzzzzzzz.*

LITTLE RED RIDING HOOD: It sure is getting to be a drag. I don't mind packing the picnic basket every time the story is told. I don't even mind taking a stroll through the woods and listening to the sounds of nature. I don't even mind helping out my poor sweet old Granny every once and a while. But when I have to deal with that furball with bad breath . . . .

CINDERELLA: He's never been nice to you. He growls at you in the woods. He outraces you to Granny's house. He steals Granny's pajamas and tosses her under the bed. And then he puts his smelly old body in her bed to wait for you to waltz in the door. It's really sickening.

SNOW WHITE: It's ugly, I tell you. Really, really ugly. He smells, he stinks, he never washes, and you have to talk with him every single time some parent or teacher tells the story. Wow, you really have it bad, girl!

SLEEPING BEAUTY: *Zzzzzzzzzzzzz.*

LITTLE RED RIDING HOOD: You know what I should do? The next time I see that stinky furball I should just walk right up to him and sock him one right in the kisser. That would teach him a lesson. I bet he'd never mess with me again.

SNOW WHITE: Yeah, right in the kisser. You'd sure show him who was boss!

CINDERELLA: Yeah, just haul off and land one right in the middle of his hairy old wolf face. By the time he woke up you'd be all the way to Granny's house, and he'd have a headache for a least a week.

LITTLE RED RIDING HOOD: Yeah, I really should teach him a lesson he'd never forget.

SLEEPING BEAUTY: *Zzzzzzzzzzzzz.*

CINDERELLA: [defiantly] Besides, you'd show him who was really in charge. Those fancy dancy writers all think that they're all soooooo smart and brilliant. They just sit around all day making up stories in which these ugly wolfy furballs attack all us good lookin' and very intelligent ladies. Obviously all the writers are males, 'cause women writers would never have some dude with a furry face and bad breath as the lead character in a story. They'd make sure that the women were all princesses and queens and all the furry males would be kept in a cage in the dungeon of some faraway castle . . . or something like that.

SNOW WHITE: Hey, I tell you what. Why don't we all get together, march right down to that deep dark forest that Red has to walk through in every story, and all teach that furball of a wolf a real lesson? What do you say?

SLEEPING BEAUTY: *Zzzzzzzzzzzzz.*

CINDERELLA: Yeah, that sounds like a great idea!

LITTLE RED RIDING HOOD: I'm all for it. Let's go.

NARRATOR: And so it was that our three heroines (nobody could wake up Sleeping Beauty) marched out of Red Riding Hood's house and into the forest. Before too long they were able to locate the wolf, who was dozing under a tree and waiting for the next story to begin. The three women surrounded the wolf and watched as Red Riding Hood punched him right in the kisser. I mean she really socked him good. Wham! Blam!! He never stood a chance. He literally staggered out of Red Riding Hood's story and into another story about some giant guy who lived at the top of a very tall vegetable. But all he could do in that story was mumble a lot and walk around in circles. He was never the same again. In his place, Red Riding Hood hired a cute little bunny and completely rewrote the ending of her story. And, of course, she lived happily ever after.

SLEEPING BEAUTY: *Zzzzzzzzzzzzz.*

THE GINGERBREAD BOY GETS BAKED
AT 350° FOR 15 TO 20 MINUTES

STAGING:

The narrator can stand off to the side. The other characters can sit on tall stools or in chairs. Gingerbread Boy does not have a speaking part.

```
        Narrator
           X                              Gingerbread Boy
                                                 X
               Little Old Woman                      Little Old Man
                      X                                    X
```

NARRATOR:	Once upon a time there was a little old woman and a little old man. They lived alone in a little old house in the middle of a little old forest in a little old country in a little old time. One day, the little old woman decided to make a little old gingerbread boy. I don't know, maybe she was thinking that the gingerbread boy would become her son one day. But how a gingerbread boy could become the son of a little old woman and a little old man is something that I just don't understand. Hey, I'm just the narrator—not some rocket scientist! Anyway, let's just say that the little old woman was just a little touched in the head—what you and I might call crazy. Anyway, on with our story.
LITTLE OLD WOMAN:	Well, now I'm finished mixing the flour, butter, sugar, ginger, and all those other ingredients. I think I'll just shape them all into a little gingerbread boy. Won't that be cute!
LITTLE OLD MAN:	Hey, Little Old Woman, why are you doing that?
LITTLE OLD WOMAN:	Because we don't have a son of our own, my Little Old Man.
LITTLE OLD MAN:	[aside to the audience] I think the narrator person is right. I think my Little Old Woman is just slightly crazy. But what do I know? Anyway, that's just the way she is, so let's just get on with the story.
LITTLE OLD WOMAN:	Never mind what that silly narrator said. I'm just going to put this little gingerbread boy into the oven and bake him

for about 15 to 20 minutes at a temperature of 350°. Then maybe we'll eat him up for dinner.

LITTLE OLD MAN: Whoa there, my loving Little Old Woman. Why would you want to eat up the gingerbread boy for dinner? Didn't you just say that maybe he could be our son?

LITTLE OLD WOMAN: Yeah, I did. Sometimes I get confused and don't know what I'm talking about. I guess I just can't make up my mind. I don't know if I really want something to eat for dinner or whether I just want to have a son.

LITTLE OLD MAN: Well, a gingerbread son would be nice. He could mow the lawn. He could wash the windows. He could sweep the driveway. He could do lots of things around here. After all, Little Old Woman, both you and I are old and little, and we can't do all the things we used to.

LITTLE OLD WOMAN: You are right, my Little Old Man. But I'm really getting very hungry. I haven't had anything to eat for a long time. And just like our friend, Old Mother Hubbard, we don't have anything in the cupboard.

LITTLE OLD MAN: Yes, you're right. There's very little to eat around this little house. Maybe we should just forget about having a gingerbread son and just eat him up as soon as he gets out of the oven.

NARRATOR: All the time Little Old Woman and Little Old Man were talking, the little Gingerbread Boy was in the oven baking away at 350°. But he was also listening very carefully to the conversation Little Old Man and Little Old Woman were having. And to tell the truth, he didn't like what he was hearing. He decided that this wasn't the place where he wanted to live. So while Little Old Man and Little Old Woman were talking away, Gingerbread Boy snuck out of the oven, tip-toed across the kitchen floor, and slipped out the back door.

LITTLE OLD WOMAN: [confused] Hey, where did our Gingerbread Boy go?

LITTLE OLD MAN: Why did he run away from us?

NARRATOR: Well, to tell the truth, Gingerbread Boy wanted to save his skin, so to speak. But he quickly discovered that life outside a 350° oven can be quite dangerous—especially when there's a fox around. He wound up having more adventures than he was ready for . . . and some of them weren't very pretty. But then again, that's another story. So now it's time to say goodbye.

LITTLE OLD MAN: [waving] Good bye.

LITTLE OLD WOMAN: [waving] Good bye.

LITTLE OLD MAN: [whispering to Little Old Woman] Say, I'm still hungry. What have we got around here to eat?

THE BOY WHO CRIED "AMPHIBIAN"
(Once Too Often, I Might Add)

STAGING:

Narrator 1 can be seated on a tall stool to the left of the staging area; Narrator 2 can be seated on a tall stool to the right. The other characters should be standing and walking around the staging area.

```
Narrator 1                                                    Narrator 2
    X                                                             X
                Villager 1      Villager 2      Villager 3
                    X               X               X
            Boy
             X
```

NARRATOR 1:	Once upon a time in a small village in a small country there was a shepherd boy.
NARRATOR 2:	Now, we should point out that a shepherd boy is a boy who takes care of shepherds.
NARRATOR 1:	No, he's not, silly. A shepherd boy is a young boy given the job of watching over a herd of sheep.
NARRATOR 2:	I've heard of sheep!
NARRATOR 1:	Not that kind of "heard." A herd of sheep is a whole bunch of sheep all in one place.
NARRATOR 2:	Oh, I get it!
NARRATOR 1:	Anyway, as I was saying . . . . There was this shepherd boy in a small village in a small country a long time ago.
NARRATOR 2:	Hey, maybe I might want to be a shepherd some day. You know, after this narrator gig I might want another job. How much money does a shepherd make?
NARRATOR 1:	[getting frustrated] I don't know and I don't care! Besides, it has nothing to do with the story we're trying to tell.
NARRATOR 2:	Oh, okay. Then go ahead.

From *MORE Frantic Frogs and Other Frankly Fractured Folktales for Readers Theatre* by Anthony D. Fredericks. Westport, CT: Teacher Ideas Press. Copyright © 2008.

NARRATOR 1:	Anyway, as I was saying . . . . There was this shepherd boy and he was asked to take care of the village flock. That is, his job was to take care of all the sheep that belonged to the village.
NARRATOR 2:	Hey, what's a flock? Can I buy one at the store?
NARRATOR 1:	No, you can't. A flock is like a group or a whole bunch of something.
NARRATOR 2:	Oh, like a whole flock of kids on the playground?
NARRATOR 1:	No, you can't have a flock of students. You can only have a flock of animals, like sheep.
NARRATOR 2:	Oh, I get it!
NARRATOR 1:	I hope you do!
NARRATOR 2:	So, there he was one day just sitting around watching these stupid sheep . . . .
NARRATOR 1:	Hey, look, sheep aren't stupid, they just don't do very much except to chew grass and mess up the lawn.
NARRATOR 2:	So the little boy was sitting around—bored out of his skull—when he got a great idea. "I'll fool the villagers," he said, "because I'm really very bored and need something to amuse myself."
NARRATOR 1:	So he yelled . . . .
BOY:	[loudly] Amphibians! Amphibians! Help! Help! Amphibians are chasing the sheep!!
NARRATOR 2:	All the villagers heard the cries of the little shepherd boy and ran up the hill to help drive the amphibians away.
VILLAGER 1:	Hey, little shepherd boy, didn't you just yell "amphibians?"
BOY:	Yes, I did.
VILLAGER 2:	Well, we just ran all the way up this hill only to find that there are no amphibians anywhere to be found.
VILLAGER 3:	Yeah, the sheep are all quietly munching on their grass and there are no amphibians anywhere. Were you kidding us?
BOY:	Why, yes I was. It just gets so boring around here watching these stupid sheep . . . .

NARRATOR 1: Now, wait a minute. Like I said before, sheep aren't stupid. So maybe they can't do three-column subtraction, but that doesn't mean they're dumb.

BOY: Anyway, it's really boring here.

NARRATOR 2: Well, all the villagers were really ticked off at the little shepherd boy for fooling them like that. And they all went back down the hill to the village, where they were all watching the latest episode of *American Idol.*

NARRATOR 1: Hey, wait a minute. This story takes place a long time ago . . . a long time ago before televisions were even invented.

NARRATOR 2: Oh, okay. Maybe they just went back to the village and sat around watching grass grow.

NARRATOR 1: Well, the boy was still back on the hill watching his sheep. And getting even more bored. So he decided to have some more fun and he yelled . . . .

BOY: Amphibians! Amphibians!! The amphibians are coming to get the sheep!!!

NARRATOR 2: I bet I know what happened.

NARRATOR 1: That's right. All the villagers ran up the hill to see what all the commotion was about.

NARRATOR 2: Yeah, 'cause they didn't want those big old hairy amphibians messing around with their cute little sheep.

NARRATOR 1: Hey, amphibians aren't hairy.

NARRATOR 2: [amazed] Oh, okay.

NARRATOR 1: So the villagers ran up the hill. But when they got to the top they just saw the little shepherd boy laughing away.

BOY: Ha, ha, ha!

VILLAGER 1: Hey, little shepherd boy. Did you fool us again by yelling "amphibians" when there were no amphibians at all?

BOY: Yes, I did.

VILLAGER 2: You know, that isn't very nice.

BOY: Yes, but it's so gosh darn boring up here with these sheep, I just wanted something to do.

VILLAGER 3:	Well, perhaps you can find a game or something. We're getting sick and tired of your stupid pranks. We can't keep running up here every time you yell something.
VILLAGER 1:	You should save your yelling for when there is something really wrong.
VILLAGER 2:	Don't cry "amphibians!" when there are no amphibians!
VILLAGER 3:	[pointing to Villager 2] Yeah, what he said.
NARRATOR 1:	With that, all the villagers went back down the hill once again. They were all pretty ticked at the little shepherd boy.
NARRATOR 2:	I bet I can guess what happened next.
NARRATOR 1:	You're probably right. The little shepherd boy saw a real amphibian prowling about his flock of sheep. Alarmed, he leaped to his feet and yelled as loudly as he could . . . .
BOY:	AMPHIBIAN! AMPHIBIAN!!
NARRATOR 2:	I bet the villagers thought that he was trying to fool them again.
NARRATOR 1:	You're right. They thought he was fooling them again. So they didn't do anything. They waited . . . and waited . . . and waited. But at sunset, everybody wondered why the little shepherd boy hadn't returned to the village with all the sheep.
VILLAGER 1:	Where's that little shepherd boy?
VILLAGER 2:	Where are our sheep?
VILLAGER 3:	Let's go see.
NARRATOR 2:	So, what did they discover?
NARRATOR 1:	The villagers went up the hill. There was the little shepherd boy, but all the sheep were gone.
BOY:	There really was a big hairy amphibian here. He came and ate all the sheep. Now all the sheep are gone. I yelled "amphibian." Why didn't you come?
VILLAGER 1:	We thought you were fooling us again.
VILLAGERS 2 & 3:	[pointing to Villager 1] Yeah, what he said.

NARRATOR 1:	So it was that the village lost all its sheep to the big hairy amphibian.
NARRATOR 2:	And I bet that there's a moral to this story, right?
NARRATOR 1:	Right! The moral is, "Never get the villagers *hopping* mad, or all your sheep may *croak*!" Get it? "Never get the villagers HOPPING mad, or [slowly] . . . all . . . your . . . sheep . . . may . . . CROAK!"

GOLDILOCKS AND THE THREE BEARS
(the Trial of the Century)

STAGING:

The narrator stands at a lectern or podium. The staging area is set up to look like a courtroom, with the judge in the middle rear, a jury along one side, two tables (one for the prosecution, one for the defense), and a witness chair. Witnesses will move back and forth between the gallery and the witness chair. The jury members have no speaking parts.

```
                        Judge        (witness chair)
                          X                 X

         Jury
         X X
         X X                                        Bailiff
         X X                                           X
         X X
         X X
         X X


      Defense Attorney   Goldilocks    Prosecuting Attorney
            X                X                  X
   Snow White                                           Narrator
      X                                                    X
                        Gallery
           X      X      X      X      X      X
           X      X      X      X      X      X
           X      X      X      X      X      X
           X      X      X      X      X      X
```

NARRATOR: Once upon a time there was this blond maiden who walked around the deep and dark forest breaking into other characters' houses. She just walked into every little cottage, dwelling, house, or castle she could find. But on this one day, she just happened to pick the wrong house. Because, you see, this house belonged to the Three Bears. So this Goldilocks character was eventually arrested and jailed for "breaking and entering." Several weeks later she was brought to trial in the courtroom of Judge Ima Wolf. We take you now to that trial.

BAILIFF:	[officially] The court will now come to order. The honorable Ima Bigbad Wolf presiding.
JUDGE:	Does the defense wish to make a statement?
DEFENSE ATTORNEY:	We do, your honor. My client has been accused of breaking and entering the Three Bears' cottage in the deep and dark forest. We will prove to this court that the Bears not only left their dwelling unlocked and opened, but actually invited my client in to try their lousy porridge, sit in their lousy chairs, and lie down in their lousy beds. After all, your honor, the Three Bears own a furniture store and had been promoting their big Thanksgiving Day sale throughout the forest for several weeks. Certainly they expected other characters and creatures to come into their place of business to try out the furniture they were selling. And the porridge . . . that was just a free promotional giveaway for the store.
JUDGE:	Thank you. Does the prosecution wish to make a statement at this time?
PROSECUTING ATTORNEY:	Not at this time, your honor. Instead, we'd like to call our first witness to the stand. We'd like to call Snow White.
GALLERY:	[mumble, mumble, mumble, talk, talk, talk]
JUDGE:	[loudly] Court will come to order. Any more outbursts like that and I'll have the bailiff clear the courtroom.
PROSECUTING ATTORNEY:	Miss White, would you please tell the court your version of the story?
SNOW WHITE:	[rambling] Well, you see, it was like this. I was over in my cottage. Actually, it's not my cottage . . . . I just happen to live there with these seven funny little men who work down at the local diamond mine and they've asked me to keep their place clean for them while they're down in the mines going "Hi, Ho, Hi, Ho, Hi, Ho" all day long. And they sing all kinds of other songs like that, which I think helps them pass the time away while they're down deep in the caverns and caves of the mine searching for the . . . .

JUDGE:	[frustrated] Miss White, would you please just tell your story?
SNOW WHITE:	Well, okay. Anyway, I was outside my cottage when I see this Goldilocks character skipping through the forest. Now I'm no "peeping tom" or anything like that, but I couldn't help noticing that she stopped at the Three Bears' cottage and looked in the window. It wasn't too long after that that I saw her open the door and walk right in.
PROSECUTING ATTORNEY:	And then what happened?
SNOW WHITE:	[rambling] Well, not too much. You see I was hiding behind a tree and I really couldn't see inside the cottage. Not that I would want to look into someone else's house, mind you. You see I'm really an upstanding citizen of the world of traditional literature and I know how to behave myself around all the other people and creatures that tend to inhabit those stories and I wouldn't want to . . . .
JUDGE:	[frustrated] Miss White, just stick to the story please!
SNOW WHITE:	Sorry, I guess I just get carried away sometimes. So after watching Miss Locks go in the house I just waited around for a while. You know, I just sorta hung out around the trees and all that.
PROSECUTING ATTORNEY:	And then what?
SNOW WHITE:	Then, the Three Bears come home. That's when I heard all the noise and fuss and commotion going on. [rambling] There was yelling, and screaming, and lots of things being said that weren't very nice . . . . I mean just because someone breaks into your house and eats all your porridge and sleeps in all your beds doesn't mean you have the right to call her a "doofiss" or a "nitwit" or a "dumb-dumb" or a . . . .
JUDGE:	Miss White, for the last time, please stay on the topic.
SNOW WHITE:	Okay, well anyway that's about all I know.
JUDGE:	Does the defense have anything to say?
DEFENSE ATTORNEY:	Yes, we do. We'd like to call Miss Gold E. Locks to the stand.

BAILIFF: Miss Locks, please sit in the witness chair.

DEFENSE ATTORNEY: Now, Miss Locks, is it true that you went into the house of the Three Bears?

GOLDILOCKS: Yes, it is.

DEFENSE ATTORNEY: What were you doing there?

GOLDILOCKS: I was just selling some Girl Scout cookies in the deep dark forest neighborhood. I knocked on the door of the Bear cottage and the door just swung open.

DEFENSE ATTORNEY: You're saying that the door opened all by itself.

GOLDILOCKS: That's right. It just opened up.

DEFENSE ATTORNEY: And then what?

GOLDILOCKS: After that, I just don't remember anything. It's all a blur. One minute I was knocking on the door and the next minute these three hairy bears were yelling things at me. I was just so frightened that I didn't know what to do.

DEFENSE ATTORNEY: Your honor, it's clear that we have someone here who is totally confused and didn't have any idea what she was doing. Sure, she may have eaten some dried up old cereal, she may have sat in some rickety old chairs that broke down, and she may have slept in some old beds that weren't very comfortable, but that doesn't mean that she's a thief. She's just a confused and frightened little girl. She's not a criminal, your honor, she's just a little girl.

JUDGE: You know what, I tend to agree. I think the whole case has been blown out of proportion. Therefore, I find Miss Goldilocks to be completely innocent. However, I would like to see the Three Bears charged with having lousy cereal around their house, equally lousy chairs, and even more lousy beds. They are an absolute disgrace to storybook characters everywhere. If there's a crime here, the Three Bears are the ones who should be charged. I want them arrested right away.

NARRATOR: And so it was. The Three Bears were charged with all sorts of crimes. They were tried and sent to jail, where they fell in with some unsavory characters like wolves, and witches, and goblins, and evil stepmothers. Eventually they all became part of this gang that would invade all kinds of stories and make the heroes and heroines look really bad. It really wasn't very pretty, but maybe some author will come along and write the true story . . . a story that will really set the record straight.

THE UGLY DUCKLING AND HIS WHOLE UGLY FAMILY
(It's a Really Ugly Story!)

STAGING:

The characters should all be standing around the staging area (stools or chairs are not necessary). Note that there is no narrator for this story.

Ugly Duckling   Ugly Sister
X   X

Ugly Father   Ugly Mother
X   X

Ugly Anteater
X

UGLY DUCKLING: [to audience] Hi, we're the Uglys. I'm Ugly Duckling.

UGLY SISTER: I'm Ugly Sister.

UGLY FATHER: I'm Ugly Father.

UGLY MOTHER: I'm Ugly Mother.

UGLY ANTEATER: And I'm Ugly Anteater. Although I'm really not sure why the writer put me in this story. I really don't live with these characters [points to others]. I just happened to be walking along eating a bunch of ants and the writer asked me if I would like to have a small part. Maybe he thought that because I was so ugly I should be in an ugly story. Go figure. I guess that writer thought that all the ugly characters should be in the same story . . . like we have nothing better to do with our time than hang around and wait for some author person to put our ugly faces in his ugly story. Can you believe that? I'm outta here [exits off stage]. [from off stage] Watch out ants, here comes Mr. Ugly, and he's really hungry!

UGLY DUCKLING: So, anyway, we're just an ugly family. Or perhaps I should say that we're a regular family. We do regular things like going on vacations, seeing some good movies, eating pizza, and having birthday parties. It's just that we're all so darn ugly.

From *MORE Frantic Frogs and Other Frankly Fractured Folktales for Readers Theatre* by Anthony D. Fredericks. Westport, CT: Teacher Ideas Press. Copyright © 2008.

UGLY FATHER: Hey, there's nothing wrong about being ugly. Ugly can be beautiful in its own special way. It's not what's on the outside that counts, it's what's on the inside.

UGLY SISTER: [sarcastically] There he goes again with that outside/inside stuff.

UGLY DUCKLING: Anyway, I guess I'm sorta the hero of this story—at least that's what the author told me. You see, a long time ago, in a country somewhere over in Europe, there lived this other writer person who wrote stories for kiddos—like you guys [points to audience].

UGLY MOTHER: Yeah, and his name was Hans Christian Andersen. He was a really cool dude 'cause he would come up with all these really neat stories about children and animals and princesses and all that stuff.

UGLY SISTER: Yeah, and one day he thinks that he should write a story about my ugly brother here [points]. Maybe he thinks that Mr. Ugly here [points] should be famous or should make a ton of money. I don't know. It just seemed stupid to me!

UGLY FATHER: So this Mr. Andersen writes a story about a family of ducks who discover that one of the brand new ducks that has just hatched out of its shell is really, really ugly. I mean he's sooooo ugly that all the other members of the family get really, really sick to their stomachs.

UGLY MOTHER: Anyway, the story goes along with all these really good looking ducks and this really ugly duckling. Then, yadda yadda yadda, it turns out that the really ugly ducking is actually a swan in disguise.

UGLY SISTER: Yeah, can you believe that—a stupid swan! A SWAN!! So then this swan turns out to be the most beautiful or handsome bird in the entire world.

UGLY FATHER: Yes, and Mr. Andersen, the writer, decides to add a little moral or lesson to the end of the story. It's something about how really ugly birds can be really beautiful birds in disguise.

UGLY ANTEATER: [from off stage] Hey, did he ever say anything about really ugly anteaters?

ALL: NO!

UGLY SISTER:	But of course you know that that was just a made-up story. Things like that don't really happen in real life. Like my ugly brother here [points] being the hero of a story and making a ton of money and all that stuff.
UGLY DUCKLING:	Yeah. I thought that Mr. Andersen was really going to make me famous. But that wasn't the case. It turns out that he just came over to our place to see what really ugly ducks looked like. I guess he just needed some models in order to be able to write his story for all the little kiddies. I really thought I was going to be the hero, but it wasn't to be.
UGLY FATHER:	Yeah, it seems like those writer people just need to get out of their offices every now and again to see what the real world looks like. Then they can go back to their computers and make up all kinds of stories with imagination and stuff.
UGLY MOTHER:	So, here's the bottom line. We are simply a very ugly family of very ugly ducks. But, you know, we're okay with that.
UGLY SISTER:	What do you mean, oh ugly mother?
UGLY MOTHER:	Well, as your father says, we shouldn't judge individuals on the outside. The real individual lies on the inside. In other words, it's what's on the inside that is more important than what is on the outside. We can't control what's on the outside, but each of us can control what's on our insides.
UGLY DUCKLING:	Like when I eat too much food and burp all the time.
UGLY FATHER:	So we're just plain ugly. In fact, we're about as ugly as you can get. But we are also very happy. We don't let our ugliness affect us because we are happy on the inside.
UGLY MOTHER:	All of our beauty is on the inside.
UGLY DUCKLING:	So I guess that means that I'm not going to have a starring role in the Ugly Duckling story.
UGLY SISTER:	No, my little ugly brother.
UGLY FATHER:	No, none of us will have a part in the movie.
UGLY SISTER:	So I guess all we can do now is go back to our ugly pond, live in all those ugly plants, eat some ugly insects for dinner, and just be happy in our very ugly lives.
UGLY DUCKLING:	Yes, we would live happily ever after.

UGLY ANTEATER: [from off stage] Hey, if you ever need an ugly movie star for the movie you could always call me. I'm not about to change—not with this ugly nose on my face and all the ugly ants I have to eat everyday. [really excited] Hey, how 'bout calling up this Mr. Andersen and asking him to write a story about the ugly anteater and how he discovers true happiness with a mouthful of ants. Wow—what a great story!!

TWO WOLVES TALKING ON THEIR CELL PHONES

STAGING:

The narrator stands to the side of the staging area. The two characters may be seated on chairs or stools. Each character may have a music stand or small table to hold the script. Each character pretends to be using a cell phone (a block of wood or a small cereal box can be used as a prop).

```
            Narrator
              X

     Wolf 1                        Wolf 2
       X                             X
```

NARRATOR: Well, here we are in "once upon a time" time again. You all know how this works. This really incredibly good looking narrator person—that's me—gets to set up a story so you know who the characters are, where the story takes place, and a little bit of the preliminary action. Why they always select all the good looking actors to do this stuff is beyond me, but here goes. You can probably see that this story has just two characters . . . yeah, that's right—just two characters who, in this case, just happen to be wolves. Well, our first wolf is someone you'll recognize instantly—he's the wolf from the Little Red Riding Hood story . . . . You know, the guy who is always terrorizing young maidens as they walk through the deep dark forest to their granny's house. Then there's our other character—the wolf guy from the Three Little Pigs story . . . . You know, the guy with an asthma problems who huffs and puffs his way across the countryside.

Anyway, those are the two characters in this script. They are both at home when Red Riding Hood Wolf decides to call his friend, Three Little Pigs Wolf. So let's listen in on their conversation. By the way, you'll probably notice that these are talking wolves . . . talking wolves who both have cell phones. Okay, I know what you're saying—how can two really hairy guys who huff and puff and sleep in granny's P.J.s have a conversation? Well, my friends, this isn't the real world—this is the world of imagination. But let's listen in anyway.

WOLF 1:   Hey, bro. How's it going?

WOLF 2: It's going fine. How be you?

WOLF 1: I be fine. Say, what's happening?

WOLF 2: No much. You know, same old, same old!

WOLF 1: Yeah, it's sorta been quiet here in the deep dark woods now that that little incident with the chick in red is over.

WOLF 2: Hey, how did that all work out?

WOLF 1: Well, you see the writers of that story made me get all dressed up in Granny's pajamas and wait for the red chick to come into Granny's house. Course that's when this dude with a gun comes along and tries to protect the red chick from me by shooting things up and yelling and screaming and stuff like that. It sure wasn't a pretty scene.

WOLF 2: Wow, those writers must have been crazy to put you in that kind of story.

WOLF 1: Well, to top it all off they made the red chick say things about my eyes, my teeth, and other parts of my body that weren't all that nice. Hey, my ego really suffered in that story. Hey, what about you and that incident with the three porkers?

WOLF 2: Yeah, wasn't that some scene? I was just minding my own business walking along the road from house to house and having me some really good pork chops for lunch when I come across this brick house. Inside there was this pig fellow with some kinda attitude problem. He was yellin' stuff at me about his chinny chin chin and all that kinda stuff.

WOLF 1: I bet you were really ticked.

WOLF 2: You bet I was. Not only that, but he also had his two brothers with him and they were yellin' stuff at me, too. They really got me agitated and all that. 'Course that's when my asthma kicked in and I started huffing and puffing and all that. 'Course that's when those silly writers came along and made me look like some bad guy trying to throw his weight around in front of some stupid little porkers. Man, I couldn't wait to get out of that scene.

WOLF 1: Hey, you know what? Seems like us wolf characters are always taking it on the chin . . . or should I say chinny chin chin. Ha, ha,ha. I mean, look what happened to me and the chick in red.

WOLF 2: Yeah, and look what happened to me and those three porkers.

WOLF 1: It seems that wolves are always getting the short end of the literary stick, so to speak.

WOLF 2: Yeah, what about our cousin—you know, the guy who dressed up in a sheep costume so he could get close to some of those fluffy critters and just eat one or two for dinner?

WOLF 1: Hey, you're right. He didn't come out too well in that story. The writers who wrote that tale made it seem like Leroy was the bad guy all along, when all he wanted was a leg of lamb for a snack.

WOLF 2: Hey, and what about all those stories where these perfectly innocent human-type people are turned into werewolves?

WOLF 1: Yeah, it makes it seem like werewolves are always bad while the people persons are always good. Oh sure, just because some hairy guys likes to sneak around on foggy nights to attack and suck the blood of innocent victims . . . it makes all of us look really bad.

WOLF 2: Hey, you know this is getting really bad. It seems like in every story with a wolf—the wolf is always the bad guy.

WOLF 1: You're right. In fact, I can't think of a single story that those writer people have written over the years that doesn't have a bad wolf in it. They're always making wolves bad.

WOLF 2: Yeah, maybe we should make up some real wolf stories—you know, stories about good lookin' wolves doin' good things.

WOLF 1: Maybe you and I could do that . . . maybe we could come up with some ideas and send them to those writer people.

WOLF 2: Okay, what do you have in mind?

WOLF 1: How 'bout this: "The Handsome Wolf Dude and the Beautiful Princess"?

WOLF 2: Or this: "The Superhero Wolf Saves the World from a Dangerous Asteroid from Outer Space."

WOLF 1: Here's one: "101 Ways to Kiss a Wolf."

WOLF 2: What about "101 Wolves You'll Really Want to Kiss"?

WOLF 1: Or this: "Wolves in Love."

WOLF 2: Or "How to Love a Wolf for Fun and Profit."

WOLF 1: Or "Wolf for President."

WOLF 2:   Or "Wolves Are My Friends, and They Don't Smell Bad, Either."

NARRATOR: And so it went far into the night. The two friends came up with all kinds of positive wolf story ideas. From "The Enchanted (and Good Looking) Wolf and the Evil Troll" to "Wolves Can Make You Rich," the two friends stopped at nothing in creating a whole bunch of new wolf stories, all designed to reveal the true nature of wolves worldwide. And you should also know that it wasn't long before some Hollywood producer contacted them to turn some of their stories into major motion pictures. Of course they both made tons of money and retired to a beach in Hawaii, where they now spend their days catching some rays and sipping iced tea in the tropical sun. But then again, maybe I should remind you that this, too, is just another fairy tale. And so, I return you now to your regularly scheduled reality . . . that's right—your classroom.

THE LION (with Attitude) AND THE MOUSE (Also with Attitude) AND THE NOT-SO-BRIGHT WRITER WHO MADE UP THIS STUPID STORY

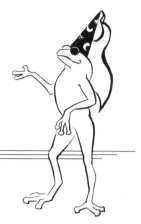

STAGING:

The narrator can sit on a stool to the front and side of the characters. The characters can sit on stools or may wish to walk around throughout the play.

	Lion	Mouse
	X	X
Narrator		
X		

LION: [upset] Okay, let's get one thing settled before we actually begin this little play here. According to the title of this story, I've got an attitude. Now, obviously that little title was written by some writer who would probably make a nice little meal for me. Oh, now don't get me wrong—it's not that I always eat writers. It's just that the little pinhead who put this story together should probably be taught a little lesson. You know, like maybe I should be nibbling on his toes, or his brain, or maybe I should just eat him in large chunks . . . very, very slowly.

MOUSE: [equally upset] Yeah, it's just my luck. I get stuck in some story with a lion who's got an attitude. You know I'm a classically trained actor, and to think that I have to waste my finely tuned acting skills playing against some beast with a temper and an eating disorder is just more than I can bear. I mean I ain't lion. Get it? I ain't lyin'!

LION: [frustrated] Oh, great, not only do I have to work with this little pipsqueak, he thinks he's some kind of comedian. That "lion" thing . . . hey, that's about as old as they come. If that's the best he can do, then I'm outta here. Geez, this is really going to be something, to work with this little weirdo.

MOUSE: [sarcastically] Yeah, like it's going to be fun for me. You know I had a big-time part in a major movie. I was going to play the part of a dashing young pirate who gets to sail around the world and plunder gold and jewels from castles and all that stuff. But then along comes this stupid writer person who decides that I should do this little script with Mr. Fuzzy face there [points at Lion]. What a waste!

LION: Yeah, like it's going to be fun for me, too! I'd rather be eating a zebra or snoring in the shade than having to do this little gig. What a drag!

NARRATOR: Okay, fans. What do you say we stop this little nonsense and get on with this readers theatre script? After all, the writer guy who put this thing together should get something for his effort. I mean, he is getting on in years—he's no spring chicken you know—so maybe we'd better just do the play and get on with our lives. What do you guys say?

LION: [reluctantly] Well, okay, if you say so.

MOUSE: [very reluctantly] I guess so. Go ahead. Let's get started.

NARRATOR: Okay, so once upon a time there was this lion [points to Lion] who was sleeping in his cave. A little mouse [points to Mouse] came along and decided to run up and down the lion's back and play with his whiskers.

MOUSE: [aside to audience] See what I mean about wasting my finely tuned acting skills?

LION: [angry] Hey, can it, you little rat! We're in the middle of this very important play.

MOUSE: [angry] Who you callin' a little rat?

LION: Me, that's who.

NARRATOR: Hey, you two. Can we just get on with this readers theatre production? I assure you . . . after we're done you two can go back to doing whatever it is you two do when you're not doing readers theatre.

MOUSE: [dejectedly] Yeah!

LION: [dejectedly] Yeah, okay

NARRATOR: So the mouse ran up and down the lion's back. But the lion woke up and caught the mouse between his paws.

MOUSE: [half-heartedly] Oh, ouch. Oh, ouch. You caught me between your paws. Please let me go and I'll come back to help you someday.

LION: [sarcastically] Yeah, right! I should just eat you right now. You'd make a great little snack.

NARRATOR: [forcefully] Hey! Let's just stick to the script, can we?

LION: Okay, okay. So anyway, little mouse, how could you ever help me? You're really so small. Ha, ha, ha.

MOUSE: Just let me go and I'll come back to help you someday.

LION: Well, okay. Good-bye, little Mouse

NARRATOR: So, the next day two hunters came into the forest.

LION: Hey, narrator person, where the heck are the two hunters? I'm lookin' around this stage and I don't see two hunters anywhere.

MOUSE: Yeah, where the heck are those hunters? I told you this was going to be a silly script. That writer person who put this whole thing together must really be off his rocker. Look! He couldn't even put two stupid hunters in the script. We're supposed to have this readers theatre production with two stupid hunters, and they're not even here.

LION: Maybe they went over to McDonalds® and hunted up some hamburgers or French fries or chocolate milkshakes or something dangerous like that. Or maybe they just forgot about the script.

MOUSE: Ha, ha, ha.

NARRATOR: Hey, you two, just cut it out. Let's get on with the script, shall we?

LION: [whispering to the audience] What did I tell you? The writer of this script must be a complete idiot. Either that or he's way too old to write readers theatre stuff, 'cause he always forgets some of the characters.

MOUSE: [aside to audience] Yeah, maybe next time we should have some young writer put this whole thing together. Those old guys don't know nothin'.

NARRATOR: [forcefully] Are you two done? Can we move on? Okay, so there were these two hunters who came into the forest, and they caught the lion in a trap made from lots of rope.

LION: [facetiously] Oh no. Oh, no. I'm trapped in a whole bunch of ropes and I can't get out. Oh, no. Oh, no. Help me. Help me.

MOUSE: Oh wise and wonderful Lion, I have come to your rescue. I will nibble on some of the ropes that are trapping you. After I nibble on enough ropes, then you will be able to escape and live happily ever after.

NARRATOR: So it was that Mouse nibbled on some of the ropes. And Lion was able to break free and run away. He was saved by his little friend.

LION: Yes, you saved me, my little friend. I was very foolish to ridicule you for being so small. You really helped me by saving my life.

MOUSE: Yes, I did. So now we can become very close friends and have lots of good times together and, like I said, we can live happily ever after.

NARRATOR: And the moral of the story is that we should not judge someone by how big or how strong he or she may be. Rather, we should appreciate the talents and skills we all have to share with each other.

LION: Okay, we've done this stupid readers theatre play. Can we get back to our real jobs now?

MOUSE: Yeah, can we get back to some writers who really know what they are doing? You know, writers who really give us finely trained actors some meaty roles with meaty lines?

LION: Come on, pal. Let's go find some real writers. What do you say?

MOUSE: I say, let's do it.

NARRATOR: And, so I am told, Lion and Mouse went to Hollywood, where they were discovered by a famous talent agent. They wound up making a ton of money. Meanwhile, the writer who wrote this little readers theatre production wound up an old man who mumbled a lot and forgot lots of stuff. But maybe you [points to audience] could visit him someday and ask him to share a story or two.

THE TOWN MOUSE AND THE COUNTRY MOUSE MEET THE SOUTHERN CALIFORNIA MOUSE

STAGING:
The narrator stands off to the side. The characters can each sit in a separate stool or chair, or they can also stand, in a semicircle, in front of the audience.

Narrator
X

         Town Mouse   Country Mouse   Southern California [S.C.] Mouse
            X   X   X

NARRATOR: Well, here we go again with another one of those "once upon a time" openings that you guys [points to audience] have been hearin' a lot of lately. But, in this story the "once upon a time" time could be any time—it could be yesterday, it could be today, or it could be tomorrow . . . but I think the writer was thinking about a time not so long ago, so let's just say that the time was just a few days ago, Okay? So, anyway, there were these two old friends—Town Mouse and Country Mouse—who were sitting out on the patio having a drink of lemonade and just catching some rays. And, I think their conversation went something like this.

TOWN MOUSE: Hey, bro. How's it going?

COUNTRY MOUSE: Not bad, my man. I mean, I'm havin' a great time just resting here with you, sipping some good old fashioned lemonade and enjoying the day.

TOWN MOUSE: Well, you weren't saying that last month. Do you remember when you came over to my pad? You had to dodge all those cars in the street, slink through some dark alleyways, leap over a couple of trash cans, and then sneak your way up a drainpipe to finally make it to my place.

COUNTRY MOUSE: Yeah, what a hassle that was. I remember saying that I never wanted to go through that again. In fact, I don't see how you stand all the noise and commotion every day. It's not like

	where I live. Of course, when you came to visit me on the farm you didn't particularly enjoy my digs too much, either.
TOWN MOUSE:	Yeah, you're right about that. I had to escape from that mean old cat that lives in the barn, watch out for all the horses and cows and all the stuff they left all over the place, and stay away from all that dangerous farm equipment that the farmer uses all the time. I thought I was going to have a heart attack. I couldn't wait to get back to my pad in the city. What a relief that was.
COUNTRY MOUSE:	Yeah, those were some days. I remember the story that those writer guys wrote about us. I think they said at the end of the story something like, "always be satisfied about where you live" or some kind of moral like that.
TOWN MOUSE:	Yeah, those writer guys are always adding some kind of moral or lesson to the end of their stories. Like they always have to teach us something.
S.C. MOUSE:	[enters from offstage] Hi, guys!
TOWN MOUSE:	Hey, where did you come from?
S.C. MOUSE:	I don't know. I was just hanging' around and all of a sudden this writer guy comes along and puts me into this story.
COUNTRY MOUSE:	Where were you supposed to be?
S.C. MOUSE:	I was supposed to be on the beach playing beach volleyball, sippin' some iced tea, and checkin' out all the action.
TOWN MOUSE:	So, what happened?
S.C. MOUSE:	I'm not sure. There I was minding my own business, when this writer guy comes along and says that he can make me a star. Well, before I could say "Yes" or "No" he just whisks me off out of my story and into this story.
COUNTRY MOUSE:	So, you really don't know why you're in this story.
S.C. MOUSE:	Right!
TOWN MOUSE:	Well, you're certainly welcome to join our story. We were just talking about old times—when we each were visiting the other. In each case, things didn't go so well—we didn't like each other's environment, so to speak.

S.C. MOUSE: Well, I'm not so sure I would enjoy it either. I guess I'm sorta spoiled. I spend all my story time catching some rays, surfin' some gnarly waves up and down the coast, hangin' 10 with my buddies, entering a couple of volleyball tournaments each summer, and having some good times with all the ladies.

TOWN MOUSE: You mean, you don't have to worry about any cats or dogs or farm equipment or pig manure or other stuff that you might find all over a farm?

S.C. MOUSE: You got that right!

COUNTRY MOUSE: And you don't have to worry about lots and lots of traffic, a couple of cats with attitude problems, and some noisy old trash cans?

S.C. MOUSE: You bet!

TOWN MOUSE: Wow, that sounds like the greatest gig in the world.

S.C. MOUSE: Well, dudes, you certainly don't see me complaining, do you? I mean, it just can't get any better than what I have each and every day. I mean, hands down, this is the greatest gig in the world. Sand, surf, and s-s-s-l-l-l-o-o-o-w-w-w summer days. It is soooooo cool!

COUNTRY MOUSE: But you know what, bro?

S.C. MOUSE: What?

COUNTRY MOUSE: I think the writers have you stuck . . . like stuck in our story.

S.C. MOUSE: What do you mean?

TOWN MOUSE: Well, I think the writers pulled a fast one on you. They wrote you into our story because we needed one more character to round out the cast. And to do that they just wrote you out of that beach bum story and into our town mouse/country mouse story.

S.C. MOUSE: Hey, wait a minute! You mean I have to give up my beach volleyball days and hangin' 10 days and cute little mice in bikinis days?

TOWN MOUSE: I think that's what the writers have in mind. I think they want you to spend the rest of your days with us.

S.C. MOUSE: Hey, just wait till I get my hands, or cute little mouse paws, on those writer guys. This isn't fair. I'm minding my own business, not hurtin' anyone, and all some writer guy has to do is write me out of my story and into your story.

COUNTRY MOUSE: That's right. I guess you're stuck with us.

NARRATOR: And so it was that Southern California Mouse was written into the story about Town Mouse and Country Mouse. His part in the Southern California story was taken over by some canine creature with lots of hair all over his body, a habit of dressing up in old lady's pajamas, and a desire to terrorize little girls wearing red hoods over their heads. I'd like to say that Southern California Mouse lived happily ever after, but I can't. I have to wait and see what kind of adventures the writer decides to get him into. Stay tuned, though. I'll be sure to get back to you on that one.

JACK AND JILL DON'T LIKE THE STUPID AUTHOR WHO WROTE THEIR STUPID STORY

STAGING:
The narrator is seated on a tall stool. The characters can be standing or seated on tall stools.

```
                                 Jack              Jill
                                  X                 X
              Narrator
                 X
```

NARRATOR: Once upon a time there were these two little kids, and their names were Jack and Jill. They would spend all day going up this stupid hill, but they never understood why. They never knew what they were supposed to do [I guess they never read the original story]. Anyway, let's listen in on one of their many conversations.

JILL: Hey, Jack. Do you know that this is about the one hundredth time we've gone up this stupid hill today? I just don't understand why the stupid author has us going up this stupid hill all the time. I mean, is he stupid or what?

JACK: Yeah, I don't understand either. Are we supposed to see something at the top of the hill? Are we supposed to get something at the top of the hill? Are we supposed to do something at the top of the hill? I'm very, **very** confused. Just what the heck are we supposed to do when we get to the top of this stupid hill?

JILL: Well, as I see it, the author wants us to go up the hill, do something at the top of the hill, and then come back down to the bottom of the hill. I don't know about you, but that sounds like about the stupidest thing I've ever heard of. I'm really getting sick and tired of going up this stupid, stupid hill.

JACK: I don't think it's the hill that's stupid—I think the author is stupid. Who would write a story about two kids going up and down a stupid hill for no reason at all? Where's the excitement? Where's the thrill?

JILL: Yeah, you're right. This story is nothing like those other stories that our friends have. You know what I mean? Like, how about the one where our friends Hansel and Gretel get to explore a really deep dark forest with that old lady who lives in the house made out of gingerbread? And how 'bout the story about our beautiful friend Cinderella who gets to go to a fancy dancy ball and meet a handsome prince who gets to put a glass slipper on her foot?

JACK: Hey, you're right. I really think we're getting cheated here. How exciting can it be to go up and down, up and down, up and down? I'm really getting sick and tired of this stupid hill and this stupid story. Hey, by the way, who wrote this story anyway?

JILL: I think it was some old lady with lots of time on her hands. I think her name was Mother Goose.

JACK: Mother Goose? What kind of stupid name is that?

JILL: I don't know. I mean, would you call your mother a goose?

JACK: I wouldn't even call my mother a frog . . . or anything, for that matter.

JILL: She must be really strange to have a name like Mother Goose. I think she's just a little weird in the head. You know what I mean? She's probably been watching too much *American Idol* or some other stupid TV show like that. After a while, her brain just turned to mush.

JACK: Yeah, maybe we should call her Mother Mushy Brain instead of Mother Goose.

JILL: Well, now what do we do? We're still stuck in this stupid story going up and down this stupid hill. And to top it all off, we have this stupid author who couldn't write her way out of a paper bag.

JACK: Hey, I know, why don't we invite some other characters over and just have one big party?

JILL: That sounds great. Maybe Big Bad Wolf would like to come. Or Snow White. Or Robin Hood and his merry men. Or Little Red Riding Hood.

JACK: Hey, wouldn't it be neat to see Little Red Riding Hood and Big Bad Wolf have a conversation?

JILL: Yeah, that would be neat.

JACK: I wonder what they would say.

JILL: I don't know, but let's start writing the invitations right now.

JACK: Didn't you forget something?

JILL: What do you mean?

JACK: It's time for us to go up this stupid hill one more time.

JILL: OH, NO, NOT AGAIN!!! That stupid author did it to us again.

JACK: Yeah, that stupid Mother Goose. What a stupid author!

JILL: Stupid! Stupid!! Stupid!!!

CHICKEN LITTLE HAS A COMPLETE MELTDOWN

STAGING:
The narrator can sit on a tall stool off to the side of the staging area. The other characters can sit on chairs or stools.

                                                    Student 1   Student 2
                                                        X   X
                            Chicken Little
                                  X
                                                    Student 3   Student 4
                                                        X   X
            Narrator
              X

CHICKEN LITTLE:	[very excited] The math homework is coming! The math homework is coming!!
NARRATOR:	Now, wait just a gosh darn minute here.
CHICKEN LITTLE:	[extremely excited] The math homework is coming! The math homework is coming!!
NARRATOR:	[impatiently] Now, just hold on, will ya? I'm trying to set up this story, and all you're doing is running around like some birdbrain. Just pipe down for a second.
CHICKEN LITTLE:	[really agitated] The math homework is coming! The math homework is coming!!
NARRATOR:	Now, wait just a gosh darn minute here. I'm supposed to be the narrator in this story, which means I'm supposed to know all there is to know about this story and other stories just like this story. So, the way I remember it, Mr. Little here [points to Chicken Little] was supposed to run around saying "The sky is falling, the sky is falling."
CHICKEN LITTLE:	[nervously] The math homework is coming! The math homework is coming!!

STUDENT 1: I think what he's saying is that, "The math homework is coming!'

NARRATOR: I know what he's saying, silly. But why does he keep saying that the math homework is coming?

STUDENT 2: Maybe he's scared.

STUDENT 3: No, I think he's just afraid of all the math homework that we get all the time. I mean, it really is a lot of math homework.

STUDENT 4: Yeah, sometimes it just takes forever to do all that homework. Problem after problem after problem after . . . .

CHICKEN LITTLE: [nervously] The math homework is coming! The math homework is coming!!

STUDENT 1: Yeah, I don't know why our teacher has to give us soooooooo much math homework. It just seems as though it never stops. It just seems like it takes forever!

STUDENT 2: Why do teachers do that? Do they really think we'll get so much smarter if we do lots and lots of math homework?

STUDENT 3: Why do they always have to pile us up with tons of math homework every night? I barely have enough time to breathe, much less time to spend on all that math homework every night.

CHICKEN LITTLE: [really agitated] The math homework is coming! The math homework is coming!!

STUDENT 4: You'd think that math homework was the most important thing in the whole wide world. Math, math, math—why do teachers have to give so much of it? Sometimes, it just never stops.

STUDENT 1: You're right. But, you know, I think we have another problem here.

STUDENT 4: What's that?

STUDENT 1: Our friend. I mean, just look at him.

CHICKEN LITTLE: [nervously] The math homework is coming! The math homework is coming!!

STUDENT 2: Yeah, I think he's really concerned about all the math homework.

STUDENT 3:	Concerned? Concerned? I guess he's just a little bit more than concerned. I think he's flipped!
STUDENT 4:	He's flipped all right. And, you know what? I think we all should be flipped. After all, just how much math homework can one teacher give? We should all be going just a little crazy.
STUDENT 1:	I heard that teachers are paid by how much math homework they give their students.
STUDENT 2:	You don't mean . . . .
STUDENT 1:	Yeah, I do mean! I overheard the principal one day. He said that teachers who give the most homework are those who get the most money.
STUDENT 3:	Why is that?
STUDENT 1:	I think it's so students will stay home and spend all their free time on the math homework. Then they won't be hanging out at the mall causing problems and listening to loud music and all that stuff that really bothers adults.
STUDENT 4:	So how does that connect with the money?
STUDENT 1:	Well, if kids are home doing lots of math homework, then the cops don't have to patrol the mall, and the city saves lots of money. The money that they save they can give to the teachers. Then everybody—at least all the adults—is happy.
CHICKEN LITTLE:	[very excited] The math homework is coming! The math homework is coming!!
STUDENT 2:	I think the whole thing stinks!
STUDENT 3:	Well, there's not much we can do about it!
STUDENT 4:	I'm not so sure. I think I have an idea?
STUDENT 3:	What's your idea?
STUDENT 4:	Listen, why don't we have our friend say something just a little different? You know, something that will get all the adults, especially all the teachers, just a little bit nervous.
STUDENT 1:	What do you have in mind?
STUDENT 4:	Just wait [walks over to Chicken Little and whispers in his or her ear].

CHICKEN LITTLE: The sky is falling! The sky is falling! The sky is falling! The sky is falling!

STUDENT 2: Brilliant! Now, with all the teachers so worried about the sky falling, they won't have time to assign all that math homework, and we'll be free to hang out at the mall and listen to loud music all the time. Brilliant!

CHICKEN LITTLE: [agitated] The sky is falling! The sky is falling! The sky is falling! The sky is falling!

ALL: The sky is falling! The sky is falling! The sky is falling! The sky is falling!

CHICKEN LITTLE: [winks and whispers to audience] See, it works. No more math homework! Ever!
[loudly] The sky is falling! The sky is falling! Yahoo! The sky is falling! The sky is falling! Yahoo!

THE TORTOISE AND THE HARE
(a Worldwide Wrestling Match You Won't Believe)

STAGING:

The two narrators are on stools on either side of the staging area. The narrators should say their lines in boastful, authoritative, announcer-type voices (they may wish to listen to voice-over announcers for sporting events on TV and model their voices accordingly). The two characters are standing facing each other. They may wish to "stalk" each other by circling around the staging area. They should speak in threatening and angry voices. The writer has a single part at the end of the script.

```
                                                              Writer
                                                                X

        Narrator 1                                          Narrator 2
            X                                                   X
                            Tortoise        Hare
                                X             X
```

TORTOISE:	Hey, your mother has hair all over her face.
HARE:	Your father has green feet.
TORTOISE:	Yeah, who says?
HARE:	I say, you dumb hardback
TORTOISE:	Yeah, we'll see who's a hardback. Just wait till I get you in the ring. I'll give you some hardback you'll never forget.
HARE:	Yeah, you and whose army?
TORTOISE:	Don't need no army, carrot-eater!
HARE:	Who's calling who a carrot-eater?
NARRATOR 1:	[in a long-drawn-out voice] L-A-D-I-E-S a-a-a-n-n-n-d-d-d G-E-N-T-L-E-M-A-N. W-E-L-C-O-M-E to tonight's main attraction. It's the match you've all been waiting for. It's the R-U-M-B-L-E in the J-U-N-G-L-E!!!
NARRATOR 2:	It's the A-N-T-S in their P-A-N-T-S!!!

NARRATOR 1: Ants in their pants!!! Where the heck did you get that?

NARRATOR 2: Sorry, wrong script. [shuffles some pages] Oh, here it is. L-A-D-I-E-S and G-E-N-T-L-E-M-E-N—the fight you've all been waiting for. The main attraction. The big kahuna. The BRAWL in ST. PAUL. The FRACUS in SECAUCUS. The BATTLE in SEATTLE.

NARRATOR 1: [slowly] These two combatants have had their words. They've had their disagreements. They've had their stare-downs. Now its time for the pedal to hit the metal.

NARRATOR 2: [slowly] IT'S TIME FOR THE MAIN ATTRACTION!!!

TORTOISE: Hey, fuzzy butt, you going to wimp out on me? You going to hide your tail between your legs and scamper off into the carrot patch?

HARE: Not a chance, helmet-head. I'm not going to hide my head under some kinda protective covering that I have to carry around with me all the time. Boy, if that's not wimpy, then I don't know what is.

TORTOISE: It's obvious you don't know much about anything. I guess that comes from eating all those carrots and hopping around like a chicken with its head cut off.

HARE: Hey, turtle breath. If there's anyone who doesn't have a head, then you're the one. Every time a little ant walks by you've got to hide your head under your shell. What a wimp!

TORTOISE: Listen, here, Mr. Hippy-hoppy. This here shell that you keep talking about is going to do some serious damage to your body. If you think you're going to be hopping outta this ring tonight, then you've got another think coming.

NARRATOR 1: L-A-D-I-E-S and G-E-N-T-L-E-M-E-N . . . in this corner, weighing in at just a little over two pounds, is BIG BAD BUNNY MAN. He's mean, he's lean, he's a F-I-G-H-T-I-N-G M-A-C-H-I-N-E.

NARRATOR 2: L-A-D-I-E-S and G-E-N-T-L-E-M-E-N . . . in this corner, weighing in at 40 pounds, is LARRY THE LOGGERHEAD. He's mean, he's lean, he's a F-I-G-H-T-I-N-G M-A-C-H-I-N-E.

NARRATOR 1 and ARE YOU READY TO RUMBLE?
NARRATOR 2:

HARE: Hey, Ocean Boy, think you're up for the challenge? Think you can take the heat? Think you can last a couple of rounds with me.

TORTOISE: Don't worry, furball. I'm not only up for the challenge, but I'm going to wupp you up so bad that it's going to take a whole hospital to put you back together again.

HARE: [sarcastically] Yeah, right! I should just teach you a lesson right now.

TORTOISE: Yeah, I should just teach you a thing or two.

HARE: Hey, beak face—you think you're so hot just because you carry a shell around with you all day long. Well, take off that shell and you're nothing but a naked reptile.

TORTOISE: You makin' fun of my species? Listen, you think that just because you've got a great pair of legs, you're the best creature in the kingdom. Hey, before this night is over I'm going to have one of your rabbit's feet hanging from my belt.

HARE: Yeah, right.

TORTOISE: Yeah, right.

HARE: Yeah!

TORTOISE: Yeah!

NARRATOR 1: L-A-D-I-E-S and G-E-N-T-L-E-M-E-N . . . the time has come. ARE YOU READY?

NARRATOR 2: ARE YOU READY?

WRITER: I'm sorry, ladies and gentlemen, but I'm going to have to cut in here. It's quite obvious that this story is getting a little too violent for all those little kiddies. I mean, we can't have a bunny and a turtle yelling at each other. And we can't have two narrator people talking in loud, boastful voices for no reason at all. This whole thing has just gotten out of hand, and I think we're going to have to change a few things so that little boys and girls and their parents and teachers don't get upset 'bout all the violence. So, I think I'll just change a few things in the plot. Maybe I'll just have a fun little game in which a cute bunny and a cute little turtle run a cute little race over the cute little countryside. And they can all live happily ever after. Now, won't that be just cute? So let me work on that and I'll get back to you with a cute final script. In the meantime, why don't you all just have a cute little day and do some cute little math problems? I'll see you later. Bye.

HUMPTY DUMPTY MAKES A LOT OF REALLY BAD PUNS

STAGING:

The reporters should all be standing around the staging area. Each can pretend to hold an imaginary microphone. Humpty Dumpty should be seated on a tall stool or chair and should speak in a silly and joking manner. The reporters should be as serious as possible. There is no narrator for this script.

Reporter 1
X

Reporter 2
X

Humpty Dumpty
X

REPORTER 1: We are gathered here at the palace of the Rich and Powerful King—Old King Cole—for this breaking story. It seems as though a Mr. Humpty Dumpty has just fallen off this very tall stone wall at the castle.

HUMPTY DUMPTY: Yeah, that's eggs-actly what happened. Get it? That's *eggs-actly* what happened. Ha, ha, ha.

REPORTER 2: According to our sources, this Mr. Dumpty climbed to the top of the wall. And because he's in the shape of an oval, he couldn't keep his balance and just rolled off.

HUMPTY DUMPTY: Hey, maybe I wasn't in my right mind. Hey, maybe I was just a little cracked. Get it? A little *cracked*. Ha, ha, ha.

REPORTER 1: According to one witness, Mr. Dumpty just splattered all over the castle floor and all over the knights and princesses.

HUMPTY DUMPTY: You got that right! The yolk was on them. Get it? The *yolk* was on them. Ha, ha, ha.

REPORTER 2: One of the witnesses said that Mr. Dumpty was in a thousand different pieces after the fall.

HUMPTY DUMPTY: Yeah, I guess they're going to have to call in some eggs-perts to try and put me back together again. Get it—*eggs-perts*. Ha, ha, ha.

REPORTER 1: This has to be one of the most serious incidents to ever happen at the castle. Nobody has ever seen anything like this.

HUMPTY DUMPTY: Yeah, I guess you could say that this is one of the most eggs-treme cases there ever was around here. Get it? *Eggs-treme* case. Ha, ha, ha.

REPORTER 2: We don't have any reports yet from the hospital, but we can only hope that Mr. Dumpty is doing well.

HUMPTY DUMPTY: Doing well! Doing well! Actually I'm in eggs-ellent shape, Get it? *Eggs-ellent* shape. Ha, ha, ha.

REPORTER 1: We're hoping to get an interview with one of the doctors or nurses at the hospital. We hope they can bring us up to date on Mr. Dumpty's condition.

HUMPTY DUMPTY: I just hope you guys know eggs-actly what you're doing. I mean, *eggs-actly* what you're doing. Ha, ha, ha.

REPORTER 2: While we're working on that angle of the story, there seems to be an unsolved mystery surrounding the case. It seems as though at least one witness saw someone push Mr. Dumpty off the wall.

HUMPTY DUMPTY: Boy, I sure do hope you guys can crack that case. Get it? *Crack* the case. Ha, ha, ha.

REPORTER 1: We have some of the finest reporters on this developing story and will report back to you as soon as we gather all the necessary information.

HUMPTY DUMPTY: I guess you guys will just have to scramble for all the information. Get it? *Scramble* for information. Ha, ha, ha.

REPORTER 2: I just hope we can find out what our viewers need to know before we go off the air today. This is truly a serious situation, and we want to be sure that you, our viewers, get all the facts.

UMPTY DUMPTY: Hey, guys, don't be so nEGG-a-tive. Get it? Don't be so *nEGG-a-tive*. Ha, ha, ha.

REPORTER 1: Hold on. I'm getting a message from the studio. It seems that we have to leave the air. I'm getting word that there's another breaking story.

HUMPTY DUMPTY: I guess their brains are fried. Get it? Their brains are *fried*. Ha, ha, ha.

REPORTER 2:   In just a moment we're going to switch you all over to our other reporters in the field. It seems as though a wolf has just entered a cottage in the woods, a cottage where a little old grandmother lives . . . and, and, and has taken the grandmother's pajamas and put them on. We don't know what's going to happen next, but we switch you now to the scene of this developing story.

HUMPTY DUMPTY: Hey, just don't egg the guy on. Get it? Don't *egg* him on. Ha, ha, ha, ha, ha, ha, ha, ha, ha, ha.

AUDIENCE: [groan]

PETER PIPER BETS THAT YOU CAN'T SAY THESE REALLY, REALLY FAST

STAGING:

There is no narrator for this script. All of the characters should be seated on tall stools or chairs. After each "run" of the script you may wish to replace the characters with a new set of students. Challenge the new set of characters to see if they can read the script faster (and more accurately) than the previous group. Be prepared for lots of laughter and fun.

	Reader 1	Reader 2	Reader 3	Reader 4
	X	X	X	X

READER 1: Peter Piper picked a peck of pickled peppers.

READER 2: A peck of pickled peppers Peter Piper picked.

READER 3: If Peter Piper picked a peck of pickled peppers,

READER 4: Where's the peck of pickled peppers Peter Piper picked?

READER 1: Betty Botter had some butter,

READER 2: "But," she said, "this butter's bitter."

READER 3: "If I bake this bitter butter, it would make my batter bitter."

READER 4: "But a bit of better butter—*that* would make my batter better."

READER 1: She sells sea shells by the sea shore.

READER 2: The shells she sells are surely seashells.

READER 3: So if she sells shells on the seashore,

READER 4: I'm sure she sells seashore shells.

READER 1: A Tudor who tooted a flute,

READER 2: Tried to tutor two tooters to toot.

READER 3: Said the two to their tutor,

READER 4:   "Is it harder to toot or to tutor two tooters to toot?"

READER 1:   A flea and a fly flew up in a flue.

READER 2:   Said the flea, "Let us fly!"

READER 3:   Said the fly, "Let us flee!"

READER 4:   So they flew through a flaw in the flue.

READER 1:   A bitter biting bittern bit a better brother bittern,

READER 2:   And the bitter better bittern bit the bitter biter back.

READER 3:   And the bitter bittern, bitten, by the better bitten bittern,

READER 4:   Said: "I'm a bitter biter bit, alack!"

READER 1:   Mr. See owned a saw.
And Mr. Soar owned a seesaw.
Now See's saw sawed Soar's seesaw

READER 2:   Before Soar saw See,
Which made Soar sore.
Had Soar seen See's saw,

READER 3:   Before See sawed Soar's seesaw,
See's saw would not have sawed
Soar's seesaw.

READER 4:   So See's saw sawed Soar's seesaw.
But it was sad to see Soar so sore,
Just because See's saw sawed Soar's seesaw!

READER 1:   How much wood would a woodchuck chuck,
If a woodchuck could chuck wood?
He would chuck, he would, as much as he could,
And chuck as much wood as a woodchuck would,
If a woodchuck could chuck wood.

READER 2:   How much wood would a woodchuck chuck,
If a woodchuck could chuck wood?
He would chuck, he would, as much as he could,
And chuck as much wood as a woodchuck would,
If a woodchuck could chuck wood.

READER 3: How much wood would a woodchuck chuck,
If a woodchuck could chuck wood?
He would chuck, he would, as much as he could,
And chuck as much wood as a woodchuck would,
If a woodchuck could chuck wood.

READER 4: How much wood would a woodchuck chuck,
If a woodchuck could chuck wood?
He would chuck, he would, as much as he could,
And chuck as much wood as a woodchuck would,
If a woodchuck could chuck wood.

OLD MACDONALD HAD A FARM
(and an Unbelievable Smelly Problem)

STAGING:

Narrator 1 can sit on a tall stool on the left side of the staging area. Narrator 2 can sit on a tall stool on the right side of the staging area. The other characters should stand and walk around as they are speaking.

```
                        Cow           Donkey
                         X              X
              Pig               Duck
               X                 X
   Narrator 1                                        Narrator 2
       X                                                 X
```

NARRATOR 1:	Old MacDonald had a farm,
NARRATOR 2:	E-I-E-I-O.
NARRATOR 1:	And on this farm he had some cows,
NARRATOR 2:	E-I-E-I-O.
NARRATOR 1:	With a moo-moo here and a moo-moo there,
NARRATOR 2:	Here a moo, there a moo, everywhere a moo-moo.
NARRATOR 1:	Old MacDonald had a farm,
NARRATOR 2:	E-I-E-I-O.
NARRATOR 1:	And on this farm he had some donkeys,
NARRATOR 2:	E-I-E-I-O.
NARRATOR 1:	With a hee-haw here and a hee . . . .
DONKEY:	Hey, just wait a gosh darn minute here! You aren't going to have me make some stupid hee haw sounds, now are you?
NARRATOR 1:	Well, that's what it say right here in the script.

From _MORE_ *Frantic Frogs and Other Frankly Fractured Folktales for Readers Theatre* by Anthony D. Fredericks. Westport, CT: Teacher Ideas Press. Copyright © 2008.

NARRATOR 2: After all, this is a very important Mother Goose story that has been around for a long time.

DONKEY: Listen, I could care less who this goosey goose lady is anyway. She may have written this story about old farmer MacDonald and his barn full of animals who make all kinds of really cute sounds and all that. But, you know what?

NARRATOR 1: What?

DONKEY: With all of us animals [points to other characters], it just plain stinks around here.

COW: Yeah, Donkey's right. That Mother Duck person, or whatever her name is . . . .

DUCK: Hey, wait a minute! That could be one of my relatives you're talking about.

COW: Hey, don't get your feathers in a tailspin. Maybe she's one of your relatives and maybe she's not. Even still, she writes some of the craziest stuff I've ever heard of.

PIG: Yeah, Cow's right! The way I hear it, she writes about cute little animals and cute little kids and cute little . . . . Well, it's all just a little too cute for me. Why doesn't she write about some of the real issues here on the farm . . . or anywhere else, for that matter?

NARRATOR 2: What do you suggest?

PIG: Well, for one, just look at where we live. You know with all us animals all over the place, there's going to be lots of . . . lots of . . . well, lots of things all over the ground.

DUCK: Yeah, and just look [points to Pig] at who is dumping most of that stuff all over the ground to start with.

PIG: Hey, lay off! Just because I'm a pig doesn't mean that I'm the dirtiest creature on the farm. Hey, I can't help it if I like to spend my days wallowing around in the mud pit. That's just the way we are. And what about you?

DUCK: What do you mean, what about me?

PIG: Well, the way I hear it, ducks aren't all that neat and tidy either. They sure do leave a lot of you-know-what all over the ground, too.

DUCK: Hey, that's not my fault. After all, all we do is eat lots of green vegetables and some grassy things.

DONKEY: Yeah, so do we donkeys. Hey, I can't help it if all I do is eat grassy things all day long and then leave grassy things all over the ground. I didn't make the rules . . . that's just the way we herbivores are.

COW: Herbivores! Herbivores!!! Wow, there he goes again using all that fancy talk. Hey, where did you get that—from reading those Mother Quack-Quack stories?

DONKEY: No, I was just paying attention in science class. Not like some of my other barnyard pals.

PIG: Hey you two—just cool it! We still have this problem all over the farm. And it still stinks. What are we going to do?

DUCK: Now look, I think we're all to blame here. Every one of us makes a mess somewhere in the barnyard, and we never clean it up. Frankly, the place just stinks to high heaven. It's gotten so bad that even old Mrs. MacDonald doesn't come out of the house anymore to collect the eggs or feed the horses. We've got to do something, and we've got to do it fast.

ALL ANIMALS: But what?

NARRATOR 1:   The animals all agreed that the barnyard was a really stinky, smelly place . . . and it was getting worse every day. But because they weren't very bright and didn't know how to use shovels . . . .

NARRATOR 2:   Maybe it was that old Mother Ducky Lucky or Goosey Loosey or whatever her name was who wrote the story in the first place who wasn't very bright.

NARRATOR 1:   Anyway, because they weren't very bright and didn't know how to use shovels, the barnyard just got smellier and smellier.

NARRATOR 2:   Eventually, the smell became so great that Mr. and Mrs. Old MacDonald had to move off the farm and into an apartment building in town.

NARRATOR 1:   Old MacDonald had an apartment,

NARRATOR 2:   E-I-E-I-O.

NARRATOR 1:   And in this apartment he had some cockroaches,

NARRATOR 2:   E-I-E-I-O.

NARRATOR 1:   With a scritch-scratch here and a scritch-scratch there,

NARRATOR 2:   Here a scritch-scratch, there a scritch-scratch, everywhere a scritch-scratch.

NARRATOR 1:   Old MacDonald had an apartment,

NARRATOR 2:   E-I-E-I-O.

NARRATOR 1:   And in this apartment he had some mice,

NARRATOR 2:   E-I-E-I-O.

NARRATOR 1:   [fading off] With a squeak-squeak here and a squeak . . .

THREE BLIND MICE GET EVEN

STAGING:

The narrator stands at a podium. The three mice sit on chairs or stools in a straight line. Note that the farmer's wife has a nonspeaking role in this script.

```
                  Mouse 1      Mouse 2      Mouse 3
                     X            X            X
      Farmer's Wife
           X
                                                        Narrator
                                                           X
```

NARRATOR: Three blind mice,
Three blind mice;
See how they run,
See how they run!
They all ran after the farmer's wife,
Who cut off their tails with a carving knife.
Have you ever seen such a . . . .

MOUSE 1:   [impatient] Hold it just a minute, buddy. Just hold it one gosh darn minute! You know, I don't know about you, but I'm getting sick and tired of always having my tail cut off whenever some teacher or class of kids says this little Mother Goose rhyme.

MOUSE 2:   Yeah, me too! Every time some class of kids in Peoria, or Portland, or Poughkeepsie says this little Mother Goose ditty, we take it on the chops, so to speak.

MOUSE 3:   Yeah, you're absolutely right. Kids sing this little song and we lose our tails . . . every time! I mean, after all, if this keeps up there's going to be a whole room full of mouse tails with no mice attached to them. [to audience] And then what are you going to do?

MOUSE 1:   To be perfectly honest, this is really getting bad. Every time we get chased by this farmer lady [points to Farmer's Wife], who runs after us with some ugly carving knife in her hands and who then proceeds to chop off our little tails. I mean, it's just not fair.

MOUSE 2:   It's really getting to be a drag.

MOUSE 3:   Maybe we should do something.

MOUSE 1:   What do you have in mind?

MOUSE 3:   Well, may be we should change the story. Instead of Farmer's Wife cutting off our tails, maybe we should be cutting off her tail.

MOUSE 2:   Hey, stupid, Farmers' Wives don't have tails. Didn't you ever notice?

MOUSE 3:   Not really, I was so busy trying to escape that crazy woman that I never got a chance to see if she had a tail or not.

MOUSE 1:   Well, take it from me, she doesn't have a tail.

MOUSE 2:   So, now what do we do?

MOUSE 1:   Maybe we should talk to our congresspeople and see if we can get some kind of law passed that prohibits farmers' wives from cutting off the tails of poor, defenseless mice.

MOUSE 3:   I don't think that's going to work. After all, those congressional types spend all their time trying to pass laws for people. I don't think they'd really have enough time for some "mouse laws."

MOUSE 2:   Maybe we should just move into another farmer's house.

MOUSE 1:   I'm not sure that's going to work, either. I'm sure that any farmer's house we move into is going to have some farmer's wife in it. And just like where we live, that farmer's wife is probably going to have an attitude problem and think that she has nothing better to do with her time than chase us around and around with some sharp instrument. You see what I mean?

MOUSE 3:   Yeah, I guess you're right. It looks like we're stuck.

MOUSE 2:   No, wait a minute! I just had a brilliant idea. Why don't we borrow a fearsome creature from another story? We could invite him (or her) over to our story and have him (or her) take care of this farmer's wife with her carving knife.

MOUSE 1:   What a great idea! Whom did you have in mind?

MOUSE 2:   Well, how 'bout Big Bad Wolf from the Three Little Pigs story?

MOUSE 3:   I don't think so. You know he's had that asthma problem for a long time, and I'm not sure he would be able to chase the farmer's wife for more than a few yards. He'd probably have to stop every so often to huff and puff and catch his breath.

MOUSE 1: Well, what about Goldilocks?

MOUSE 2: GOLDILOCKS!!!

MOUSE 1: Yeah. Remember how she used to break into all those cottages in the woods? She'd break in and eat all their cereal, crush all their chairs, and mess up all their beds. When the occupants would come home, the whole cottage would be messed up by that Goldilocks girl. I mean, they would really be ticked off.

MOUSE 3: There's only one problem with Goldilocks. You know she is a blond. And you know what that means. After all, do we really want a blond working for us?

MOUSE 2: Okay, how about an evil stepmother or a troll from under the bridge or a fire-breathing dragon. Surely we can find one of them around here to help us out.

MOUSE 1: Yeah, they would be great to have on our side. The only problem is that they are all part of the "Weird and Ugly Monster's Union," and they would have to charge us a whole lot of money before they would even think of chasing after that farmer's wife.

MOUSE 2: So it looks like we're stuck with that crazy old lady.

MOUSE 3: Yeah, I guess we are.

MOUSE 1: Well at least we're getting our exercise every time some class of kids reads that stupid Mother Goose rhyme.

MOUSE 3: Yeah, you're right about that.

MOUSE 2: So I guess we're just stuck—run, old lady, whack . . . run, old lady, whack . . . run, old lady, whack.

MOUSE 1: Whack . . . whack . . . whack!

MOUSE 3: Whack . . . whack!

MOUSE 2: Whack!

NARRATOR: Three blind mice,

Three blind mice;

See how they run,

See how they run!

They all ran after the farmer's wife,

Who cut off their tails with a carving knife.

Have you ever seen such a sight in your life

As three blind mice,

Three blind mice,

Three blind mice?

SOME CHARACTERS SUE THE STORYTELLERS OVER THEIR REALLY WEIRD NAMES

STAGING:

The narrator sits in the front of the staging area—to the left or right side. The other characters can be seated on stools or may be standing throughout the presentation.

Yankee Doodle [Y.D.]   Little Red Riding Hood [L.R.R.H.]
X   X

Humpty Dumpty [H.D.]   Goldilocks [G.L.]
X   X

Narrator
X

NARRATOR: Good morning, ladies and gentlemen. Today I would like to introduce you to some familiar characters—these are all characters you have met in stories before. But today these characters seem to have a gripe—something that really seems to be bothering them. It seems as though . . . .

Y.D.: . . . Bothering us! Bothering us!! BOTHERING US!!! You bet your little pinhead it's been bothering us!

NARRATOR: Hey, don't get your nose all out of joint! This is supposed to be a civilized readers theatre production—not an opportunity for you to rant and rave and get all excited.

Y.D.: Hey, little narrator person, let's get something straight. You may be sitting there on your fancy dancy chair or stool or whatever you want to call it. But those of us here are the real workers in this production. All you have to do is sit on your big you-know-what and just read some really nice words to all the people [points to audience] out there.

NARRATOR: Hey, slow down. You don't have to get your tail feathers in a knot. What seems to be the big problem here?

L.R.R.H.: Problem! Problem!! You bet it's a problem. For one, just look at our names.

NARRATOR: What about your names?

From *MORE Frantic Frogs and Other Frankly Fractured Folktales for Readers Theatre* by Anthony D. Fredericks. Westport, CT: Teacher Ideas Press. Copyright © 2008.

L.R.R.H.:	Well, Mr. Not-So-Bright-Narrator-Person. Just look at how stupid our names are. I mean how many people do you know walking around who have the last name "Red Riding Hood"?
NARRATOR:	Well, I have to admit, I really don't know anybody with a last name like that.
L.R.R.H.:	Yeah, and how 'bout my first name? If that isn't an insult, then I don't know what is.
H.D.:	She's right. Look at me. How many folks do you know who have a last name "Dumpty"?
NARRATOR:	Ahhhh, well, no one really.
H.D.:	Yeah. Just imagine how I feel whenever I have to fill out a job application or sign my name in a book about my life. I can just hear everyone laughing themselves silly when they find out my name is Mr. Dumpty. All the kids make fun of me, like, "Hey, Mr. Dumpty, do you really live in a dumpy?" or "Hey, Dumpty Dumpty, how come you're so lumpty, lumpty, lumpty?"
NARRATOR:	Well, I can imagine it could get a little tiresome after a while.
G.L.:	Yeah, and what about me? Who was the really stupid storyteller who gave me my stupid name? You know what, he was probably so stupid that he forgot to give me a last name—all I have is a first name.
NARRATOR:	And that bothers you?
G.L.:	You bet your big knock knees it bothers me. Everyone thinks that just because I'm a blond they can call me "Goldilocks." And then there are all the "dumb blond" jokes.
NARRATOR:	What do you mean?
G.L.:	Well, how about this one. Why did the dumb blond stare at the can of frozen orange juice?
NARRATOR:	I don't know.
G.L.:	Because it said "concentrate."
AUDIENCE:	HA, HA, HA.
G.L.:	Hey, you [pointing to audience]—just can it!

Y.D.: So you can see we're all stuck with these really stupid names. Everybody makes fun of us. Nobody understands us. And we're ashamed to go anywhere in public.

NARRATOR: So what do you plan to do?

L.R.R.H.: Well, for one, we plan to sue those stupid storytellers who gave us these stupid names. I mean, they must be about the stupidest people in the whole stupid world.

H.D.: Yeah, they must all just sit around a big stupid table drinking lots of stupid coffee and seeing what kinds of stupid names they can come up with for all the characters in all those stupid stories.

G.L.: How stupid is that? Pretty soon there'll be characters with names like "Twinkle Toes," or "Miss Hairy Arms," or "Mr. Doesn't Know the Capital of North Dakota."

Y.D.: Yeah. Just look at how stupid my name is. Yankee Doodle. Every time I go out someone always says, "Hey Mr. Noodle!" "Or is that 'Mr. Oodles of Noodles?' Or is that 'Mr. Doodle Doodle Doodle?' " You know, it gets pretty tiring after a while. Everybody thinks they're a comedian—especially when they get to make fun of your name.

NARRATOR: So, are you still thinking about suing the Storytellers' Union?

L.R.R.H.: You bet we are!

G.L.: Maybe we'll stop working in all those stories!

H.D.: Maybe we'll just walk right out of the library and not show up whenever the librarian has a story time for all the little kiddies.

Y.D.: Or maybe we'll charge everyone lots of money whenever they do use our names. That will get them thinking carefully about how and when they can just use our names.

L.R.R.H.: How 'bout a dollar every time someone uses our names?

H.D.: No, how 'bout five dollars each time someone says one of our names?

G.L.: I know, let's make it easy for us and easy for everybody else. Forget the money. Let's just all get new names.

ALL: Yeah, that sounds great!

NARRATOR: So what will your new names be?

Y.D.: Well, my new name could be "Bob."

L.R.R.H.:   My new name could be "Karen."

H.D.:   My new name will be "Jeff."

G.L.:   And my new name is "Kim."

NARRATOR: Well, there you have it folks. Thanks for coming. Be sure to come back next week, when we'll present another readers theatre script. Our story next time will be all about Jeff.

Y.D.:   Jeff, Jeff, sat on a wall.

L.R.R.H.:   Jeff, Jeff, had a great fall.

G.L.:   All the king's horses and all the king's men,

H.D.:   Couldn't put Jeff [points to self and smiles] back together again.

NARRATOR: Good night!

THE BIG BAD PIG AND THE
THREE LITTLE WOLVES

STAGING:

The narrator sits on a tall stool. The three wolves and the pig should be standing.

```
                                          Third Wolf
                                              X
                                Second Wolf
                                    X
                     First Wolf
    Narrator            X                              Big Bad Pig
       X                                                    X
```

NARRATOR: Everybody's heard the story about the Three Little Pigs. You know, the one about how they wanted to build their houses out of straw, or sticks, and even bricks, and then this big bad wolf guy with really bad breath comes along and tries to blow all their houses down, but he can't blow the last house down because it was made by the smartest pig brother, and so the wolf falls into a big pot of boiling water, and the pig brothers live happily ever after, yadda, yadda, yadda. Remember that one? Well, that's not the real story, because the real story was actually about a couple of teeny tiny wolves and this really ugly and enormous pig who really loves to eat wolf burgers and wolf chops and then . . . .

BIG BAD PIG: [frustrated] Hey, Mr. Talks-a-lot, let's get on with the story already. We don't have all day, you know. Some fancy shmancy storyteller might want to use us in some other story, you know, and we can't keep him waiting.

NARRATOR: Okay, okay, I was just trying to tell our friends here [points to audience] about the origins of our little story here. Unlike you, I wasn't trying to ham it up. Get it? Ham it up!

BIG BAD PIG: [irritated] I'll ham you up, narrator-face. Now let's get on with the tale.

NARRATOR: Gee, some guys just don't know how to have fun. Anyway, where was I? Oh, yes, now I remember. So, as I was saying, there were

From *MORE Frantic Frogs and Other Frankly Fractured Folktales for Readers Theatre* by
Anthony D. Fredericks. Westport, CT: Teacher Ideas Press. Copyright © 2008.

these three teeny tiny wolf characters who were walking down the road one day. So, let's listen in.

FIRST WOLF: Hey, brothers, it looks like we're lost.

SECOND WOLF: You're right. I guess we better stop and build a house for the night.

THIRD WOLF: Okay, let's get started.

NARRATOR: Each of the teeny tiny wolves goes off to hunt for materials with which to build his house. Now at this point in the story, it's important that you know that two of the three wolves are not as smart as your everyday wolf. In fact, they're really pretty dumb. If it wasn't for their smart brother, they'd all be in a whole lot of trouble. But listen in and you'll see for yourself.

FIRST WOLF: I'm going to build a nice three-story house out of these weeds I found by the river.

SECOND WOLF: Are you crazy? Do you know what can happen? A big bad pig could come along and blow your house down.

THIRD WOLF: Well, brother, what are you going to use to build your house?

SECOND WOLF: I found thousands and thousands of dried leaves in the forest. I'm going to build an enormous town house in the middle of the forest.

BIG BAD PIG: Maybe I should step in here and say something. I think you [points to audience] can all see that the first and second wolves in this little story are not the brightest things on four feet. Actually, they're really quite dumb. In fact, I think they're dumber than dumb. They're just plain stupid. So, I'm thinking to myself, do I really want to waste my precious time with these two incredibly dumb wolves? After all, they are teeny tiny, so they aren't going to have a whole lot of meat on their bones—certainly not enough to fill me up. And, of course, they're not very smart. I don't know if I should even waste my time with them.

THIRD WOLF: [to audience] I guess it's time for me to step in here. This guy [points to pig] is really beating up on my two really stupid bothers. He thinks that they're skinny and that they're dumb. And he's probably thinking that they're not going to make much of a meal.

BIG BAD PIG: [to Third Wolf] Hey, it's not just that. I just want to know how I ever got into this story in the first place. After all, I'm an accomplished actor. I've got good looks! I have muscles rippling all over my body! I'm one handsome dude! I mean, why should I be wasting my time with some really stupid wolves?

THIRD WOLF: Hey, we're not all stupid!

BIG BAD PIG: That may be true, but just the same, I'd rather be on some California beach with some great-lookin' actress in a new movie. Why should I waste my time with you guys?

THIRD WOLF: Because that's what the storyteller wrote for you.

BIG BAD PIG: Just wait till I get my hands on that stupid author.

NARRATOR: And so it was that the story about Big Bad Pig and the Three Little Wolves never was finished. Later Big Bad Pig went on some reality TV show and the Three Little Wolves retired to a farm in Pennsylvania, where they spent their time chasing after sick sheep. Along came some new movie makers, and they changed the characters into three pigs and a single bad wolf and made a lot of money. But that's the way it always is in Hollywood. The End.

LITTLE RED HEN GETS REALLY TICKED OFF AT ALL HER FRIENDS (P.S. She's Not a Happy Camper!)

STAGING:

The narrator can be seated on a stool to the side of the staging area. Little Red Hen can be standing, and the other characters can be seated on stools. Little Red Hen may move around among the characters.

```
                         Cat    Dog    Pig
                          X      X      X
             Little Red Hen
                  X
                                              Narrator
                                                 X
```

NARRATOR: Once upon a time there was a Little Red Hen who lived with her chick babies in the barnyard. She worked hard every day cooking for her children, doing the laundry, washing the floors, and lots of other stuff that chicken mothers do for their chicken babies. Now, this Little Red Hen had three friends—a cat, a dog, and a pig. Hey, don't ask me—I don't know why she would want to have a pig as a friend. I'm just telling the story. I mean, it doesn't make sense to me why she would want to have a pig as her friend. I mean, after all, what can pigs do—they just wallow in the mud and grunt all day long.

PIG: Hey, just a piggy minute here. Let's just stop making value judgments about Little Red Hen's friends. Just tell the stupid story and move on.

NARRATOR: Okay, okay, don't get your little piggy tail in a knot. Anyway, as I was saying, she had these three friends. But these three friends never did anything. They just sat around every day drinking lemonade, watching MTV, and swatting flies while Mrs. Little Red Hen was busy taking care of her chicken babies and her chicken house. Her three lazy friends just sat around doing nothing. Just a bunch of lazy bums, if you ask me.

CAT: Hey, big mouth narrator. Just for the record, we're not asking you. Just tell the story and let's get on with it. Okay?

NARRATOR: Okay. Anyway, one day Little Red Hen was out working in her garden. As she was pulling up some weeds, she noticed some grains of wheat on the ground. Now don't ask me where those grains of wheat came from—maybe they fell out of the sky or maybe the writer of this script just put them there so he would have a story to share with you guys [points to audience]. Anyway, there were these grains of wheat that Little Red Hen found on the ground.

LITTLE RED HEN: Who will help me plant this wheat?

CAT: Not I.

DOG: Not I.

PIG: Not I.

NARRATOR: So Little Red Hen planted the wheat herself. The wheat grew and grew. Little Red Hen took care of the wheat. She watered it, she pulled all the weeds out, and she hoed the ground. Finally the wheat was ready to be harvested.

LITTLE RED HEN: Who will help me harvest the wheat?

CAT: Not I.

DOG: Not I.

PIG: Not I.

NARRATOR: So Little Red Hen worked very hard—from morning till night—to harvest all the wheat. She loaded all the wheat on her little red wagon and took it into town. When she got to town she went to see the miller. The miller ground all the wheat into flour. She went back home with all the flour, and there were her three friends.

LITTLE RED HEN: Who will help me bake the bread with this flour?

CAT: Not I.

DOG: Not I.

PIG: Not I.

LITTLE RED HEN: Now wait a gosh darn minute here. You guys have got to be the laziest, most apathetic, and most passive characters I ever seen in a readers theatre play. I mean, you guys are beyond lazy. You can't or you won't do anything. You never help me out, you never do any work around here, and you never ever raise a finger, or paw, to contribute to this farm.

CAT: Hey, back off chicken lady! In case you haven't noticed, I'm a cat. Sure, I have four feet and four paws, but that doesn't mean I can sweep the floor or do the laundry. And now you want me to grind some stupid wheat. Hey, let's get real!

DOG: Yeah, and what about me? Sure, all I do all day long is drool and bark and drool and chase cats and drool and take long naps and drool and sniff other dogs. You must think I've got some sort of talent—like watering wheat plants or harvesting stupid wheat plants or other stuff like that. Hey, I'd rather use my talents in other ways.

PIG: Look, Chicken Lady, I'm just like my friends here; well, not exactly like my friends. I may be messy and sloppy, but at least I'm better looking than they are. And besides, how am I supposed to water some wheat plants or grind some wheat plants into grain or take some stupid flour from those wheat plants and turn it into loaves of bread? I've got hooves on the end of my pink little feet. It's not like I've got hands like you.

LITTLE RED HEN: [angrily] Hey, hold on a minute here. You guys are really beginning to tick me off. All I hear is lots of complaining and moaning and groaning. You guys do nothing except complain. You don't offer to help. You don't give me any slack. You depend on me to do all the work around here, and all I get is your lousy complaints. Hey, guys, get a life! I'm not your servant, you know.

CAT: Hey, take it easy Mrs. Chick Chick—don't have a coronary! What about us? You know, we may just be getting sick and tired of you ordering us around all the time.

DOG: Yeah, Cat's right! All you do is tell us what to do. Do this, do that, do this. That's all you say. You're like some kinda dictator.

PIG: Yeah, Dog's right! You MUST be a dictator. What gives you the right to order us around? This isn't your farm, you know. Old MacDonald probably has a thing or two to say about who runs this place.

LITTLE RED HEN: [very angry] BUZZ OFF! TAKE A FLYING LEAP! GO JUMP IN THE LAKE! Now, you've really got me angry. You're all just a bunch of lazy, no-good bums. You just think I should do everything around here without any help from you three slobs. SLOBS,

SLOBS, SLOBS! All you guys are is a bunch of slobs! A bunch of lazy no-good slobs!

CAT: Well, if that's the way you feel about it . . . .

DOG: I can't believe it comes down to this . . . .

PIG: I never. I never . . . .

NARRATOR: And so, Little Red Hen gets really ticked off. I mean, she REALLY GETS TICKED OFF! In fact, she's not a happy camper. She decides that she can't take it any more and packs up her bags and her little chicken children and leaves the farm. Unfortunately she takes a wrong turn on her way to the city and winds up in front of a local KFC restaurant. The rest of the story, I'm sad to say, is not very pleasant. So maybe we'd better stop right here.

DON'T KISS SLEEPING BEAUTY
(and the "Equal Time" Response)

STAGING:
The narrator stands off to the side. The characters can each sit on a separate stool or chair. They may wish to stand in a circle in front of the audience, too. You may wish to consider having all five parts played by boys (see the note after this script).

```
            Narrator
               X

                  Prince 1    Prince 2    Prince 3    Prince 4
                     X           X           X           X
```

NARRATOR: Now here's another story that also happened a long time ago. I guess that's just the way it is with fairy tales; they all seem to have taken place in the "good old days"—you know, the days before microwave ovens and cell phones. Anyway, once upon a time, there was this incredibly beautiful princess who was so good looking that all the princes from miles around wanted to marry her. She was one gorgeous lady. Now in order to make this story interesting, we have to have an evil character. In this story, it's a wicked witch who gets the incredibly beautiful princess to eat some kind of semi-poisoned food, and the princess immediately falls into a deep sleep. The witch makes the mistake of tossing the poison bottle in the town garbage dump. One of the local princes finds it and notices that the antidote to the poison is a kiss from a handsome prince.

PRINCE 1: Wow! All I have to do is kiss Sleeping Beauty and she will awaken from her sleep to be my bride.

NARRATOR: [to the prince] That's right, Prince 1.

PRINCE 1: Hey, guys. You're not going to believe this, but that Sleeping Beauty woman is sound asleep in that small cottage at the edge of the enchanted forest just waiting for one of us to stop by and give her a kiss that will wake her up.

PRINCE 2: Well, why didn't you kiss her?

PRINCE 1: Well, it seems as though our fair maiden has bad breath. I mean really bad breath! It was so bad that all the flowers in the house had wilted and the wallpaper was peeling off the walls. WHEW! Boy, did it stink!!!

PRINCE 3: You mean, you didn't kiss her after all?

PRINCE 1: No way, José. I couldn't even get in the room. I mean, even the flies were dropping like flies!

PRINCE 4: That's unbelievable. Here's this incredibly gorgeous princess, sleeping like a baby in the cottage just down the road, and we can't even get close enough to kiss her. Wow, what a waste!

PRINCE 1: Yeah, and just as bad is the fact that she snores like a bear. Every time she breathes the windows rattle and the dishes in the kitchen crack and break. You'd have to be crazy to want to live with a woman like that. Not only will her breath make your skin peel, but her snoring is enough to wake up the dead.

PRINCE 3: Boy, that's unbelievable!

PRINCE 1: If you think that's bad, you should see what all the animals in the forest are doing. They're packing up and leaving in droves. Not only is she stinking up the air, but she's making the whole neighborhood shake with her snoring. It's getting to the point that nobody wants to be within five miles of the small cottage at the edge of the enchanted forest.

PRINCE 2: Well, how are we going to wake her up? Doesn't somebody have to kiss her, marry her, and live happily ever after in order for this story to end the right way?

PRINCE 1: Hey, maybe you pal, but not me! If you want to go ahead and kiss old "Hog's Breath," then help yourself. As for me, I'm going over to the next forest and see if I can get a date with Snow White; that is, if she's not going out with Grumpy, or Sneezy, or Dopey, or someone.

NARRATOR: And so it was that nobody wanted to kiss Sleeping Beauty. It wasn't until many years later, when mouthwash was invented, that a traveling salesman finally had the nerve to pour some mouthwash into Sleeping Beauty's mouth. He kissed her and she finally woke up. But of course she couldn't marry him because he wasn't part of the original story. So she spent the rest of her life living in the forest with a few squirrels and talking to lizards.

NOTE TO TEACHER OR LIBRARIAN: After students have performed the script above, invite them to perform the one on the following pages. In this case, you may wish to have girls assume the roles of all five characters.

STAGING:

The narrator stands off to the side. The characters can each sit on a separate stool or chair. They may wish to stand in a circle in front of the audience, too.

Narrator
X

Princess 1   Princess 2   Princess 3   Princess 4
X   X   X   X

NARRATOR: Once upon a time there were these princes. Now it should be mentioned that these princes were not the brightest guys you ever met in your life. They probably had a lot of things rattling around in their heads, but those things certainly weren't oversized brains. Every time they would walk down the street they would trip over their shoelaces, stub their toes, or bump their heads on some brick walls. They would hang around the corner looking at all the good looking princesses who always walked downtown and talk about how some day they hoped to kiss one of those beautiful princesses. It wasn't because there was some evil stepmother or wicked witch who cast a spell over these little pinheads, it was just that they were . . . well, let's just say that they were not too bright. But, maybe I'd better let my friends tell you the story.

PRINCESS 1: Hey, girls, how about that story that you just heard?

PRINCESS 2: You mean the one about Sleeping Beauty who had bad breath and all the prince guys wanted to come up and try to kiss her, but they decided that she had really bad breath so they didn't kiss her after all?

PRINCESS 1: Yeah, that's the one.

PRINCESS 3: What kinda stupid story was that? You know, Sleeping Beauty's a nice kid. She's one of us—tall, gorgeous, blond, and beautiful. Those prince guys must be stupider than rocks if they think she's got bad breath.

PRINCESS 4: Yeah, I know for a fact that she uses the best mouthwash in the kingdom. Her teeth sparkle and her breath is like the sweet smell of honey. Bad breath! Ha! Those guys don't know what bad breath is.

PRINCESS 1: Yeah. Maybe they should kiss a warthog or a vampire bat or a gorilla with attitude.

PRINCESS 2: Yeah, those prince guys must think they're the hottest thing in the whole kingdom. I mean, come on, get real! They're just a bunch of lazy slobs who just sit around all day watching a bunch of sports and getting their feet all over the furniture.

PRINCESS 3: Yeah, just a bunch of lazy bums, if you ask me!

PRINCESS 4: I mean, what good are they? They're messy. They're sloppy. They're just plain pigs. Yeah, pigs!

PRINCESS 1: And here's another thing. Why is it that those sloppy prince guys always get the best parts in these stories? Why are the stories and fairy tales and legends always told from the male point of view?

PRINCESS 2: Yeah, Princess 1 is right. All those fairy tales and stuff always have the guys as the heroes or main characters. I mean, look at Jack and the giant—both men.

PRINCESS 3: And look at Humpty Dumpy. Also a man . . . a big fat round man . . . but a man, nonetheless.

PRINCESS 4: And what about the Three Little Pigs? Who's the main character in that one? That's right—a male wolf.

PRINCESS 1: So, ladies, what do you say?

PRINCESS 2: I say let's chuck all those sloppy princes.

PRINCESS 3: I say let's get those writers to write more stories with females as the main characters.

PRINCESS 4: I say let's not do any more stories until all those sloppy princes get a job and we get some respect around here.

NARRATOR: And so it was that all the male characters were out of a job—at least as far as fairy tales and legends were concerned. Eventually, along came some female writers who created strong female characters like Cinderella and Snow White and Rapunzel and all the others. And, as you might imagine, the result was that everyone lived happily ever after. Well, except for the princes. They had to wash all the dishes in the castle and dust all the furniture. [sarcastically] Oh, what a bummer!

THE READERS THEATRE SCRIPT AT THE END OF THIS PART OF THE *MORE* FRANTIC FROGS . . . BOOK

STAGING:
The characters can all be seated on tall stools or chairs. Note that there is no narrator for this script.

Little Red Riding Hood   Cinderella   Goldilocks   Jill (no Jack)   Little Bo Peep
X   X   X   X   X

LITTLE RED RIDING HOOD: Well, ladies, it looks like this book is almost complete.

CINDERELLA: Hey, I had a great time!

LITTLE BO PEEP: Yeah, so did I!

JILL (NO JACK): Me too!

LITTLE BO PEEP: So, the only thing left is to do this little readers theatre script that the teacher gave us.

LITTLE RED RIDING HOOD: I guess she (or he) really believes in readers theatre.

GOLDILOCKS: [innocently] Yeah, you got that right!

JILL (NO JACK): Well, I know one thing. I learned lots of neat stuff.

CINDERELLA: Yeah, me too.

GOLDILOCKS: Yeah, you know what I learned?

LITTLE BO PEEP: No, what?

GOLDILOCKS: [coyly] I learned that even really old teachers who use readers theatre scripts can be totally cool!

JILL (NO JACK): Hey, wait a minute. Where did that come from?

GOLDILOCKS: [innocently] W-E-L-L-L-L-L-L-L-L, it says so right here in the script [point to script].

CINDERELLA: So, if it says so in writing, then it must be right?

GOLDILOCKS:	That's what I always learned.
LITTLE BO PEEP:	Me, too!
LITTLE RED RIDING HOOD:	Well, anyway . . . you know what else?
JILL (NO JACK):	No, what?
LITTLE RED RIDING HOOD:	Did anyone happen to notice the teacher? [everybody looks and then points]
LITTLE BO PEEP:	I didn't notice that before. She's (or he's) really smart!
GOLDILOCKS:	Hmmmm, I wonder if it's true of all teachers who use readers theatre in their classrooms?
CINDERELLA:	I think you might be right.
LITTLE BO PEEP:	I don't see why not.
JILL (NO JACK):	Or, maybe our teacher is really a former frog now married to an enchanted person, who took up using readers theatre scripts to stop the evil fire-breathing dragon from giving students way too much math homework.
GOLDILOCKS:	No, sillies, [rapidly] it means she (or he) likes to include readers theatre as an essential element in any elementary language arts program, because it enhances the development of fluency skills, which have been shown through many research studies to be a critical element in the overall reading growth of youngsters. And, besides . . .
ALL:	WHAT?
GOLDILOCKS:	It also means that readers theatre . . . and the people who write it, are both . . . well . . . are both . . . really intelligent!
CINDERELLA:	You know what, I think she's right . . . sorta. After all, just look at all the good stuff we learned today.
LITTLE BO PEEP:	Yeah, we learned that readers theatre fosters curiosity and enthusiasm for literature.
JILL (NO JACK):	It also stimulates the imagination and helps students think in divergent ways.

LITTLE RED RIDING HOOD: Hey, don't forget that it helps kids become more confident and self-assured.

CINDERELLA: And let's remember that it also helps students learn about some of the major features of children's literature.

GOLDILOCKS: And it's fun to do, too! Well, I mean, at least the people who write those scripts are fun people!

LITTLE RED RIDING HOOD: Well, there you have it. Readers theatre can be a valuable element in any classroom or library.

CINDERELLA: I think we can all agree on that. But now how do we end this script?

LITTLE BO PEEP: Gee, I don't know.

JILL (NO JACK): Neither do I!

GOLDILOCKS: I do. Why don't we nominate this teacher [points] for Teacher of the Year?

LITTLE RED RIDING HOOD: What a great idea!

CINDERELLA: Hey, I really like that. So how can we do that?

JILL (NO JACK): Well, why don't we do what it says right here in the script [points to script]?

LITTLE BO PEEP: Wow, aren't we a brilliant group!

GOLDILOCKS: Okay, I'll talk to the principal and make sure he or she knows about it.

LITTLE RED RIDING HOOD: Yeah. And I'll talk to all the people on the school board and make sure they know about it, too.

CINDERELLA: Yeah, and I'll talk to the reporters at the newspaper and make sure they write articles about it.

LITTLE BO PEEP: This is really cool.

JILL [NO JACK]: Yeah, it sure is. But, wait a minute.

LITTLE RED RIDING HOOD: What?

LITTLE BO PEEP: What if everyone thinks that this is just another fairy tale?

CINDERELLA:	You're right! They might think that we just made up this whole story—just like the author of *MORE Frantic Frogs and Other Frankly Fractured Folktales for Readers Theatre* made up all those stories that we just did.
GOLDILOCKS:	Do you think they'd really think that?
CINDERELLA:	They just might.
LITTLE BO PEEP:	So now what do we do?
LITTLE RED RIDING HOOD:	Well, I guess maybe we should just say that we're the coolest class in the whole school and just leave it at that.
CINDERELLA:	Yes, that's what we should do.
LITTLE BO PEEP:	Yeah, we have a cool teacher and we've done some cool scripts and we've had a cool time and we learned lots of cool stuff and . . . .
JILL (NO JACK):	And that's cool!
GOLDILOCKS:	I'm cool with that! But let's not forget—readers theatre is . . .
LITTLE RED RIDING HOOD:	Educational!
CINDERELLA:	Inspirational!
LITTLE BO PEEP:	Wonderful!
JILL [NO JACK]:	And fun!
GOLDILOCKS:	And especially don't forget that classes who use readers theatre are cooler than cool. [Everyone face the audience and wave goodbye.]
ALL:	Goodbye!

Part III
FROG CENTRAL—A REALLY HOPPING PLACE

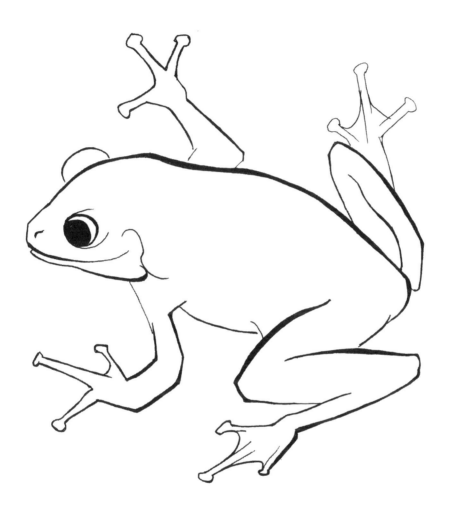

A HUNKA, HUNKA FROG PRINCE

STAGING

The narrator stands and may walk from frog to frog with a makeshift microphone. Each of the frogs is on a stool or sits on a chair.

Frog 1   Frog 2
X   X

Frog 3   Frog 4
X   X

Narrator
X

NARRATOR: [to audience] Welcome to "Make a Date with a Frog," the show that matches willing and eager young froglets with the man, er, excuse me, the frog of their dreams. Each of the young froglets in our studio today has been looking for a hunka, hunka frog prince for quite some time. Let's find out more about them. [to characters] Tell, me, Frog 1, what are you looking for in a frog prince?

FROG 1: I'm looking for someone with big lips. I want a frog who really knows how to eat all those flies swarming around the swamp all day long. Frog princes with big lips really turn me on.

NARRATOR: And what about you?

FROG 2: Well, for me a frog who has a really long tongue is what I'm looking for. I just want a guy who can sit on his lily pad and snap a fly out of the air with one zip of his tongue. But he's got to be fast. I just can't stand those slow-tongued frog princes. They're really not good for anything.

NARRATOR: Hmmmm, sounds interesting. And, what about you, Frog 3?

FROG 3: For me, my prince has to know how to leap. I mean, he's got to have some really well-developed legs. I don't want anyone with wimpy legs—those legs have got to have power in them . . . yeah, real muscles in those froggy's legs is what is really going to get me excited. If he can't hop, I don't want anything to do with him.

From *MORE Frantic Frogs and Other Frankly Fractured Folktales for Readers Theatre* by Anthony D. Fredericks. Westport, CT: Teacher Ideas Press. Copyright © 2008.

NARRATOR: That all sounds very interesting. But what about you, 4?

FROG 4: Well, for me, I really don't care what he looks like, or how far he can hop, or even what he eats for dinner. I think the thing that really gets me all excited about a frog prince is if his skin is all covered with lots and lots of slime. That's right, slime. I don't want some guy with dry skin. Ohhhhhh, that just turns me off. He's got to have a nice thick layer of slime allllllll over his body. He's got to be covered from head to toe—excuse me, from frog lips to frog legs—with nice gooey, slippery, slippery slime. If he don't have the slime, then I don't have the time.

FROG 1: Hey, you know what, 4 is right!

FROG 2: Yeah, hey, who really cares about a guy's lips?

FROG 3: Yeah, and who really cares if he can snap some stupid flies out of the air?

FROG 1: Yeah, you know, I think 4 has the right idea. When it all comes down to it, a guy with slime all over his body has got to be the coolest thing ever!

FROG 4: Yeah, I can't think of anything I'd rather do than cuddle up with some frog prince all covered with slime. Ohhhh, my heart just tingles when I think of that.

FROG 1: Yeah, slime, slime, slime!

FROG 2: If he don't have the slime . . .

FROG 3: . . . then I don't have the time.

FROG 4: All together now.

ALL FROGS: If he don't have the slime, then I don't have the time.

FROG 4: One more time!

ALL FROGS: If he don't have the slime, then I don't have the time.

NARRATOR: [to the audience] Everybody!

AUDIENCE: If he don't have the slime, then I don't have the time.

NARRATOR: Again!

AUDIENCE: If he don't have the slime, then I don't have the time.
If he don't have the slime, then I don't have the time.
If he don't have the slime, then I don't have the time.
If he don't have the slime, then I don't have the time.

NARRATOR: Well, there you have it, ladies and gentlemen. All frogs, especially these lovely frogs here on our stage, agree that if a frog prince wants a date with a lovely froglet, then he's gonna have to be covered with lots and lots of slime. It's slime, ladies and gentlemen. That's right—S-L-I-M-E!

ALL FROGS: [loud] If he don't have the slime, then I don't have the time.
[normal voice] If he don't have the slime, then I . . . .
[softer] If he don't have the . . . .
[whisper] If he don't . . . .

THE TOADS DEMAND EQUAL TIME

STAGING

The narrator sits on a tall stool. The characters should all be standing and may elect to walk around throughout the production.

Toad 1
X

Toad 2
X

Toad 3
X

Frog
X

Narrator
X

NARRATOR: [rambling] For most of your lives you've probably heard lots of stories about frogs. You probably heard all those stories about Kermit the Frog and his friends down at the swamp. And you've probably heard those stories about the frogs who lived on lily pads when they were really enchanted princes just waiting for some princess to come along and kiss them to break an evil spell put on them by some wandering witch. And you've probably heard all those stories about . . . .

TOAD 1: [impatiently] Hey, can we just get on with this story?

TOAD 2: Yeah, you know this isn't your story. It's OUR story!

TOAD 3: Yeah, it's our story. So why don't you just bug out and leave the rest of the story to us. Okay?

NARRATOR: Hey, don't get your shorts all in a bunch. I'm fine with what I've done. So why don't you guys just go ahead and tell your little story.

TOAD 1: [defiantly] Okay, we will! Anyway, here's how our little story goes.

TOAD 2: You see, we were getting just a little sick and tired over all those cute little frog stories. I mean, every story you ever heard coming out of those silly fairy tales and old fashioned legends was about some enchanted frog.

From *MORE Frantic Frogs and Other Frankly Fractured Folktales for Readers Theatre* by Anthony D. Fredericks. Westport, CT: Teacher Ideas Press. Copyright © 2008.

TOAD 3: Yeah, frogs, frogs, frogs! I mean, after all, you can only talk about frogs for so long. What's so special about frogs? Oh, sure, they have some cute legs and all that. And they can hop around from lily pad to lily pad. But, after that, what else can they do?

TOAD 1: Yeah, 3's right! They may be green and all that, but there are lots of green critters that are very good looking. I mean, just look at us. [to audience] Aren't we just the handsomest dudes you ever saw?

TOAD 2: And those frog characters always get the best parts in movies and plays and all those other readers theatre scripts. I mean, who's writing those stories anyway?

TOAD 3: So we thought that it might be a good idea to have a couple of stories starring us—you know, the cutest and brightest and smartest and best-looking and nicest and bravest and all-around handsomest critters you ever saw . . . in this swamp or anywhere else for that matter.

TOAD 1: So we decided to hire some of the best writers in Hollywood.

TOAD 2: And we told them to write us a story that would really make us shine . . . one that would put us right on the map . . . right where we belonged.

TOAD 3: So these very expensive writers began to write their epic story. And it wasn't too long before they showed us the first draft. And were we delighted and amazed!

TOAD 1: It was the best story ever. They turned us into super creatures—handsome devils who got all the good looking ladies and handsome devils who got all the money and lived in very expensive pads down by the swamp.

TOAD 2: Yeah. It was a fantastic story. Loads of Hollywood directors wanted to turn it into a blockbuster movie.

TOAD 3: And those people who make all those really cool video games wanted to turn it into a flashy and wild video game.

TOAD 1: We were so happy that we were just hopping all over the place.

TOAD 2: But then something happened. But maybe we'd better turn the story over to our friendly neighborhood narrator. Okay?

NARRATOR: Okay. You see the toads had this really cool story that had been put together by the finest team of writers in all of Hollywood. There was lots of action and lots of other stuff that I can't tell you just right now, but it's really cool. But then someone, remembered something. Everybody had forgotten one very important fact . . . one fact that would make all the difference in the world.

TOAD 3: Yeah, it made all the difference.

TOAD 1: We were sad.

TOAD 2: We were mad.

TOAD 3: It was really, really bad.

FROG: I guess maybe I should tell you what it was. You see, in all the excitement and in all the writing that was taking place, everyone forgot one thing. They forgot that toads can't read. So the toads couldn't do their movie, they couldn't star in those video games . . . . In short, they couldn't do anything.

NARRATOR: So, all the toads just hopped on back to the swamp and spent the rest of their days sharing warts with each other. And they didn't live happily ever after.

THE FAMOUS MOVIE ACTRESS
AND THE KISSING LESSON DOWN
AT THE POND

STAGING

The narrators are at a lectern or podium near the front of the staging area. The frogs are in the background and can be on chairs or tall stools. Famous Movie Actress and the princesses can walk around as they say their lines.

NOTE: You may wish to use the name of a currently popular movie actress or singing phenom in place of "Famous Movie Actress." Invite students to suggest possible names.

```
Frog 1              Frog 2              Frog 3
   X                   X                   X


                 Princess 1
                     X
        Famous Movie Actress              Princess 2
                 X                            X
                 Princess 3
                     X
     Narrator I      Narrator II
        X               X
```

NARRATOR 1:	[very seriously] The story we are about to bring you is true. The events happened just as you will see them. Only the names of the amphibians involved have been changed to protect the innocent. It happened one day at a place not too far from here—in a time not too long ago.
NARRATOR 2:	Now, since you are a very bright and very intelligent audience you probably know that in "once upon a time" time there were a bunch of castles, and these castles were always located in areas with poor drainage—today referred to as swamps. And always in the swamps there were all sorts of creatures, including frogs, trolls, wicked witches, and an occasional toad or two. Well, for our purposes today, we're not going to worry about the trolls and other strange individuals, since they have absolutely no part in this story. Instead, we're going to focus

exclusively on the amphibious members of our friendly neighborhood pond.

NARRATOR 1: [very seriously] And it's all true—100 percent absolutely and positively true . . . just as you are about to see it.

NARRATOR 2: And so, because you are a very bright and very intelligent audience, you also know that in those "once upon a time" days the local castles were filled with beautiful princesses. And because the princesses had nothing better to do with their time than sit around and watch flies walk across the ceiling, they would frequently saunter down to the local pond and do something positively disgusting! [pause]

PRINCESS 1: Look, we read in some of those other "once upon a time" stories that there were a bunch of really cool princes down at the pond—all cleverly disguised as frogs.

PRINCESS 2: Yeah. And we heard from our local neighborhood sorcerer that all we had to do was to kiss the right frog and he would be turned back into a handsome dude of a prince and we could marry him and live happily ever after.

PRINCESS 3: The only thing our friendly neighborhood sorcerer didn't tell us was how to distinguish the enchanted frogs from the nonenchanted frogs. I mean, once you've seen one frog you've seen them all. Right?

ALL FROGS: Ribbit! Ribbit! Ribbit!

PRINCESS 1: So, quite naturally, all we could do was to kiss each and every frog in the pond [the frogs all make unpleasant faces].

ALL FROGS: Ribbit! Ribbit! Ribbit!

PRINCESS 2: And I'm telling you, if you've ever tried to kiss a couple dozen frogs . . . . It's not the most sanitary thing I've ever done.

ALL FROGS: Ribbit! Ribbit! Ribbit!

PRINCESS 3:	But that wasn't the worst of it. After we had kissed about a hundred of these precious little creatures, we discovered something truly amazing—they didn't have lips. That's right, these slimy little critters [points to frogs] had no lips whatsoever!
PRINCESS 1:	Yeah. And have you [points to member of the audience] ever tried to kiss someone who doesn't have lips? It's like trying to kiss a scrambled egg—it's mushy and gooey and slimy and it's just plain not fun!
PRINCESS 2:	And the worst thing is they just don't do anything. They just sit there on their lily pads while we have to get down on our hands and knees, bend over into some kind of pretzel shape, and plant a big juicy one right on their mouths.
ALL FROGS:	[very excitedly] Ribbit! Ribbit! Ribbit!
PRINCESS 3:	We finally realized that we weren't getting anywhere. We kissed just about every lipless frog in the swamp, but nowhere could we find our enchanted princes. I mean, it was a real bummer!
NARRATOR 1:	[very serious] The preceding story has been absolutely true. But the next part of the story is even more absolutely true.
NARRATOR 2:	Now, as was the custom in "once upon a time" time, there was one character in the story who was more intelligent and certainly more beautiful than all the other characters put together. In this story that character is Famous Movie Actress. Now, Famous Movie Actress wasn't your everyday average movie actress. No, siree. On one hand she was the epitome of loveliness—she was beyond pretty, she was beyond attractive, she was beyond gorgeous, she was beyond incredibly stunning, she was beyond . . . . .
ALL FROGS:	Hubba. Hubba. Hubba.
NARRATOR 1:	Well, anyway, I think you get the idea. And not only was she the most ravishing thing in the entire kingdom, she was also the brightest. In fact, she was beyond bright, she was beyond intelligent, she was beyond brilliant, she was beyond . . . well, anyway I

	think you get the idea. But perhaps we'd better let Famous Movie Actress tell her side of the story.
FAMOUS MOVIE ACTRESS:	Well, finally! All I've been doing for the last several minutes is stand around inside this story with nothing to do or nothing to say. Now I get my big chance.
PRINCESS 1:	So, Famous Movie Actress, what do you think we should do about this kissing situation, or perhaps, I should say—lipless frog situation?
FAMOUS MOVIE ACTRESS:	Well, I've been around, and sure I've kissed a few lipless amphibians in my time . . . and a few other lipless creatures that I won't go into now. And they're all pretty much the same.
ALL FROGS:	[very quietly] Ribbit! Ribbit! Ribbit!
PRINCESS 2:	So, Famous Movie Actress, what did you do? What can we do?
FAMOUS MOVIE ACTRESS:	What you need to do is find that one special amphibian—the one who's different from all the others . . . the one who stands out . . . the one who's distinctive, singular, and unique.
PRINCESS 3:	We've tried that, Famous Movie Actress, but they all look the same—they're all slimy . . . they've all got webbed feet . . . they've all got big, bulging eyes . . . . I mean, the reality is that once you've seen one you've seen them all.
PRINCESS 1:	What you mean is that once you've kissed one you've kissed them all.
FAMOUS MOVIE ACTRESS:	Ahhhhhhhh. But I'm not just talking about frogs. Remember there's always more fish in the sea, or should I say—there's always more amphibians in the pond?
PRINCESS 2:	Hey, I'm not as bright and not as pretty as you. What exactly are you trying to say?
FAMOUS MOVIE ACTRESS:	What I'm saying, girls, is this—you need to expand, you need to cast a wider net, you need to go out and beyond, you need to . . . . What I'm saying is, you need to kiss something besides just frogs.

PRINCESS 3:	Wow, we never thought of that. We were always told that the enchanted princes took the shape of frogs. Wow, were we mistaken.
FAMOUS MOVIE ACTRESS:	That's right, Princess 3. Don't forget that there are many different kinds of amphibians besides just frogs. Myself . . . well, I've dated a few salamanders, gone out with a couple of toads, and even held hands with a newt.
ALL PRINCESSES:	[amazed] Ohhhhhhhhhhhhhhh!
FAMOUS MOVIE ACTRESS:	But you've got to be careful. Because if you ever do find that enchanted amphibian and he turns into a prince person, you know what happens?
ALL PRINCESSES:	No, we don't. Please tell us.
FAMOUS MOVIE ACTRESS:	Well, after you kiss them, all they want to do is hang around and get fat and lazy and never pick up after themselves and never do the housework and always burp and watch stupid football games, and so on and so on.
ALL PRINCESSES:	[amazed] Ohhhhhhhhhhhhhh!
PRINCESS 1:	So, what's your advice, Famous Movie Actress?
FAMOUS MOVIE ACTRESS:	Easy, just remember this—you can kiss them, but you don't have to take them home.
NARRATOR 2:	[knowingly] Ain't that the truth!

THE ORIGINAL HIP-HOP (by Busta Frog)

STAGING

There is no narrator for this script. The characters should all be standing around in a loose arrangement. Encourage the characters to sing (not read) their lines in a typical hip-hop fashion. They may also want to get "in character"—walking and acting as some of their favorite musical artists might. You may wish to play a musical accompaniment in the background.

Singer 1   Singer 2   Singer 3

X   X   X

SINGER 1:   We're gonna sing you this song,
And it won't take long.
It's about some creatures,
With real ugly features.

SINGER 2:   Not cats or dogs,
But leap leapin' frogs.
They're hip, they hop,
They jus' can't stop.

SINGER 3:   Now their skin is green,
And it makes 'em look mean,
But, don't you scare,
'Cause they be fair.

SINGER 1:   Now these dudes all hang,
In the swamp in a gang.
And they make loud sounds,
In the night on their rounds.

SINGER 2:   They sing and they croak,
In the pond where they soak.
They ribbit through the night,
And they ribbit real tight.

From *MORE Frantic Frogs and Other Frankly Fractured Folktales for Readers Theatre* by Anthony D. Fredericks. Westport, CT: Teacher Ideas Press. Copyright © 2008.

SINGER 3:   They flip their tongue,
                    Both the old and the young.
                    And they catch big flies,
                    That flitter through the skies.

SINGER 1:   Now mos' of the time,
                    Their skin be slime.
                    It don't bother me none,
                    'Cause they be havin' fun.

SINGER 2:   Now come one day,
                    This writer did say,
                    These frogs need some glory,
                    These frogs need a story.

SINGER 3:   So he wrote a frog tale,
                    And he made a frog sale,
                    'Bout a princess and a prince,
                    In a time that's long since.

SINGER 1:   See, this dude he was a frog,
                    Who was livin' in the bog.
                    A witch she cast her spell,
                    And turned his life to hell.

SINGER 2:   He hopped from pad to pad,
                    And he ate some flies—not bad.
                    But he wanted to get out,
                    Of that he had no doubt.

SINGER 3:   So, a princess came along,
                    A rockin' to her song.
                    She looked across the place,
                    And a smile it crossed her face.

SINGER 1:   What if I kiss a frog,
                    In this damp and dirty bog?
                    Perhaps a prince he'll be,
                    And then he'll marry me.

SINGER 2:   So, she kissed mos' every one,
                    Till the day was almos' gone.
                    But the prince she didn't find,
                    And she nearly lost her mind.

SINGER 3: A thousand frogs she kissed,
In the damp and swampy mist.
And her lips most all the time,
Was planted on their slime.

SINGER 1: But she never found that dude,
In the leaping froggy brood.
He had left this swampy place,
For a swingin' hip-hop place.

SINGER 2: He had hitched a ride to town,
There was action goin' down.
No more flies to bite,
He was groovin' every night.

SINGER 3: And so our story's told,
'Bout a frog who's brave and bold.
He be hippin' and a hoppin',
Ain't no way this frog be stoppin'.

ALL: And the princess she be sad,
For the froggy prince she had.
Every day and all the time,
She still be kissin' slime.

THE TONGUE-TIED FROG (Not a Pretty Story)

STAGING

The narrator stands and may walk from character to character with a makeshift microphone. Each of the characters is on a stool or sits on a chair.

NOTE: Freddy Frog ("The Tongue-Tied Frog") says his lines in a most unusual way. This character must stick out his or her tongue and then hold the end of the tongue tightly between his or her thumb and index finger. The characters' lines are then said while holding the tongue in this manner.

Freddy Frog
X

Farrah Frog   Felicia Frog
X   X

Fly Guy
X

Narrator
X

NARRATOR: We now take you down to "Frog Central," where this late-breaking story has just come in. It seems as though there is a certain frog in Swampville, USA, who has a very serious problem. I mean, this is really very serious. Let's interview some of the participants and see what's going on. Excuse me, would you mind if we talked with you?

FARRAH FROG: Not at all. You see, we were just down here at the swamp hangin' out when we noticed something unusual.

NARRATOR: What do you mean, "unusual"?

FARRAH FROG: Well, you see we have this friend—Freddy Frog. And he's a cool dude and all that. But one day we noticed that he has a little trouble saying things.

FELICIA FROG: It's not like he's got some speech problem. It's just that he . . . well . . . he . . . well, it seems as though he got a little tongue tied.

NARRATOR: Tongue tied! What do you mean?

FELICIA FROG:	Well, maybe we'd better let Freddy tell you.
NARRATOR:	Okay. Hey, Freddy, what seems to be the problem?
FREDDY FROG:	[holding his tongue] The problem seems to be that I can't speak in the normal way that a frog should speak.
NARRATOR:	How do you mean?
FREDDY FROG:	[holding his tongue] Well, I just can't speak the way I used to. It's almost like my tongue was tied up in knots.
NARRATOR:	How did it get that way?
FREDDY FROG:	[holding his tongue] Well, one day I was just minding my own business when along comes this big juicy fly.
FLY GUY:	That's me!
FREDDY FROG:	[holding his tongue] Anyway, this fly comes along and I'm really hungry you see. I want to eat him for dinner.
FLY GUY:	That's right. We flies are always getting chased around by frogs who have nothing better to do with their time than eat us poor defenseless little creatures.
NARRATOR:	Then what happened?
FREDDY FROG:	[holding his tongue] I was about to whip out my beautifully designed tongue when . . . all of a sudden . . . it wouldn't work.
NARRATOR:	What do you mean?
FARRAH FROG:	I think he means that his tongue wouldn't whip.
NARRATOR:	Maybe we should hear it from him.
FREDDY FROG:	[holding his tongue] So, I tried and I tried and I couldn't get my tongue to work right.
FLY GUY:	Boy, was I relieved! For the first time in my life I got a frog with a tongue problem. I was sure thankful! Yes, I was!
NARRATOR:	Then, what?
FREDDY FROG:	[holding his tongue] Well, I had to go to the tongue doctor. She looked at my tongue and said that it was all tied up. Well, I knew that already. So I asked her why I had a tied-up tongue.
NARRATOR:	What did she say?

FREDDY FROG: [holding his tongue] She said that I had been working too hard. She said that I was probably trying to catch too many flies. I may have tried to whip my tongue at some fly passing by and I may have strained a muscle.

NARRATOR: A strained tongue muscle. That must have hurt.

FREDDY FROG: [holding his tongue] Yes, it did.

NARRATOR: What did she tell you then?

FREDDY FROG: [holding his tongue] She told me that I couldn't catch any more flies. It would probably be too dangerous and might further strain my tongue.

NARRATOR: So now what happens?

FREDDY FROG: [holding his tongue] Well, I had to find something soft to eat while my tongue was healing. So I went over to the "Little Miss Muffet" story and borrowed some of her curds and whey.

NARRATOR: You what?

FREDDY FROG: [holding his tongue] I borrowed some of her curds and whey. It's pretty disgusting stuff, but it will have to do. Hopefully, in about a week or so I'll be back to normal and will be able to snag as many flies as I want.

NARRATOR: [to audience] There you have it, ladies and gentlemen—the true story of the tongue-tied frog and his new diet of curds and whey. Stay tuned for further events, which we'll bring to you as soon as possible. Good night and good luck!

Part IV

STORIES THAT THE AUTHOR OF THIS BOOK DIDN'T (or Couldn't) FINISH (But Maybe You and Your Students Can)

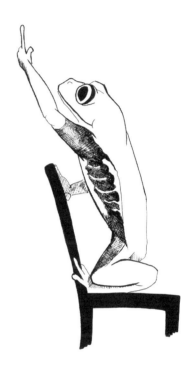

Now, I don't want you to get the idea that your friendly neighborhood readers theatre author is lazy (crazy—yes; lazy—no). It's just that for many authors—particularly those who are getting along in years—it takes a long, long time to write a book. After months and months of drafting creative, dynamic, and very humorous stories and scripts, a writer (particularly one getting up in years) tends to get a little—how should we say this—fatigued and worn out. So, the writer tends to cut corners—like forgetting to include apostrophes in all those contractions; ignoring essential prepositions like "on," "beyond," and "after"; and writing a whole bunch of incomplete sentences. And then there's all that business about defending some storybook characters who are accused of "breaking and entering" certain cottages in the woods, the little incident with the evil stepmother and her penchant for poisoned fruit, and, let's not forget, trying to quash that rumor about the frogs with slimy lips and the princess who just couldn't stay out of trouble (you know who we're talking about).

So, as you can see, being a readers theatre author is hard work—there are lots of responsibilities and lots of tasks to attend to all the time. This is why some readers theatre authors (particularly the ones getting along in years) tend to tire just a little more easily than those readers theatre authors who have recently graduated from college or have been teaching for just a couple of years and have all their faculties intact and haven't lost any brain cells due to all the various characters they have to keep track of because they are frequently getting into trouble or are having some behavioral problems that need to be addressed (Hint: Never invite the giant who lives at the top of Jack's beanstalk to the same party as the witch who lives in the gingerbread house in the middle of the deep dark woods. Let's just say this—it's not a pretty sight!).

So, anyway, where were we? Oh, yes, now I remember. We were taking about how some (getting along in years) authors have trouble finishing the parts of a book that appear near the end of that book. And believe it or not, this is where you (or your students) come in. You see, this section of the book has a bunch of unfinished readers theatre scripts. These stories are designed to serve as starters for your students' self-created readers theatre scripts. In other words, have students use one of these as the beginning or opening for a readers theatre story they may want to create. Students can add to them, modify them, or alter them in accordance with their own warped sense of humor, the rise and fall of the tides, circadian rhythms, the beat of a different drummer, or whatever else "floats their boat." Watch out though; you're about to have a classroom or library overflowing with lots of grins, giggles, and guffaws (and what the heck is a guffaw?).

So, while you and your students are working on these unfinished scripts, I think I'll just lie down for a while and take a short nap (this writing stuff is tiring—especially for us authors who are getting along in years). But, anyway—have fun!

MOTHER GOOSE FOR PRESIDENT

STAGING:
The narrator stands to one side of the staging area. The characters can all sit on chairs. If possible, place a small table in the center of where the characters are sitting.

```
              A-Person              B-Person
                 X                     X
                        (table)

              C-Person              D-Person
                 X                     X
    Narrator
       X
```

NARRATOR: Not so long ago, in "once upon a time" time, a bunch of people were eating breakfast at their local coffee shop. They were talking about all the things that were happening in the world as well as all the things that were happening in this country. Before too long the conversation turned to politics.

A-PERSON: You know what? I'm getting tired of all these politicians promising this and promising that. They just sit around on their fat you-know-whats and don't do anything at all.

B-PERSON: You're absolutely right! Those guys couldn't find their way out of a paper bag. They have got to be dumber than dumb.

C-PERSON: Absolutely! Like you said, they don't do anything. They're incompetent, they're lazy, and they're good-for-nothing.

D-PERSON: You know what we need? We need a leader who will not only get the job done, but really knows how to work with all kinds of characters.

A-PERSON: I know just the individual. How 'bout Mother Goose?

ALL: MOTHER GOOSE!!!

From *MORE Frantic Frogs and Other Frankly Fractured Folktales for Readers Theatre* by Anthony D. Fredericks. Westport, CT: Teacher Ideas Press. Copyright © 2008.

A-PERSON: Yeah, good old Mother Goose. Look, for one, she really knows how to deal with all kinds of characters. For example, she can deal with that sneaky wolf in the Red Riding Hood story.

B-PERSON: Yeah, and she knows just what to do in emergencies like, when some big round guy falls off a wall and gets splattered all over the sidewalk.

C-PERSON: Yes, and wasn't she the one who sent Jack and Jill up the hill to do a very dangerous job?

D-PERSON: Yeah, and she was also the one who discovered Little Boy Blue asleep under the haystack and really made him pay for it.

A-PERSON: You know what? I think we've got a great candidate here for president. What do you think?

POSSIBLE CONCLUSIONS

1. Cinderella and Snow White come into the coffee shop with some campaign literature about "Little Jack Horner for President."

2. Mother Goose begins her campaign for president and promises to read stories to everyone in the country every night.

3. The Brothers Grimm come over and things really start to turn ugly.

4. Big Bad Wolf huffs and puffs and blows the coffee shop down.

5. Your idea.

THE WIND (a.k.a. "Mr. Blowhard") AND THE SUN (a.k.a. "Mr. Hotstuff")

STAGING:

The two main characters can be standing in the middle of the staging area. They may wish to walk around as necessary. The narrator should be on a tall stool or chair off to one side of the staging area. Note that the man does not have a speaking part, but he should have a coat or jacket on throughout most of the play.

```
        Narrator
          X

              Mr. Blowhard          Mr. Hotstuff
                  X                      X
                          Man
                           X
```

NARRATOR: Once upon a time the wind, also known as "Mr. Blowhard," boasted of his great strength. He told everyone that he was the strongest force anywhere to be found. In fact, he said that he was the strongest force that there ever was. But the Sun, also known as "Mr. Hotstuff," argued that he was stronger. He said that he had much more power than did Mr. Blowhard. But let's listen in to what they say.

MR. BLOWHARD: You know, I'm the strongest thing there ever was. Why, I have more strength than anyone could ever imagine. I can be found in the power of hurricanes and cyclones and tornadoes and all kinds of stuff. You know, they don't call me Mr. Blowhard for nothing.

MR. HOTSTUFF: Well, that may be. But I think that I have so much more power than you do. I have some pretty hot temperatures. I can radiate my strength all over the entire universe. My light can be seen for millions of miles around. Indeed, I have the most power of anyone.

MR. BLOWHARD: I think you're just full of hot air!

MR. HOTSTUFF: And I think that you're an old windbag.

From *MORE* *Frantic Frogs and Other Frankly Fractured Folktales for Readers Theatre* by Anthony D. Fredericks. Westport, CT: Teacher Ideas Press. Copyright © 2008.

MR. BLOWHARD: I'm stronger!

MR. HOTSTUFF: No, I'm stronger!

MR. BLOWHARD: Oh, yeah!!

MR. HOTSTUFF: Yeah!!

NARRATOR: And so it was that Mr. Blowhard and Mr. Hotstuff decided to have a contest to see who had the most power. When they both looked below, they saw a man walking along a road. He was wearing a warm winter coat.

MR. HOTSTUFF: As a test of strength, let us see which of us can take the coat off that man.

MR. BLOWHARD: That sounds simple enough. I think that I shall go first.

POSSIBLE CONCLUSIONS

1. During the contest, Mr. Blowhard is approached by an agent and is signed to do broadcasts for the Worldwide Wrestling Federation.

2. Mr. Hotstuff asks the planet Jupiter out on a date, and they go out to another solar system.

3. The man gets really tired of being blown around and all the hot temperatures and decides to go inside his house and download songs on his iPod.

4. The narrator goes berserk and runs around the room yelling, "The sky is falling, the sky is falling!"

5. Your idea.

GOLDILOCKS AND THE SEVEN DWARFS

STAGING:
The narrator should be on a stool on the side of the staging area. The other characters can all be standing or standing behind music stands.

                                                          Narrator
                                                             X

      Goldilocks   Bear 1   Bear 2
          X   X   X
              Grumpy   Sneezy
                 X   X

NARRATOR: I should tell you right before we begin that this is sorta a strange story. Its not that the story is strange, it's just that one of the characters is really, really strange. In fact, I think she's really, really confused. She's so confused that she doesn't even know how she got into this story . . . or any story for that matter. But maybe we should let her tell the story.

GOLDILOCKS: You see, one day I was just minding my own business. In fact, I was minding my own story—you know the one—the one about me romping through the forest and peeking into the windows of that cute little cottage development and occasionally breaking into one or two of them to snack on some warm porridge and all that stuff.

GRUMPY: [aside to Sneezy] Gee, she sure does ramble a lot. I think she must have eaten some kind of poisoned apple from another story.

SNEEZY: Oh, you mean that poisoned apple from the Snow White story?

GRUMPY: Yeah, that's the one.

GOLDILOCKS: So, there I was minding my own business when something really strange happened.

BEAR 1:   What was really strange was her. I mean, she just waltzes through our development sticking her big nose into our cottage and . . . .

BEAR 2:   . . . and thinking that she just owns the place. [sarcastically] Yeah, right!

BEAR 1:   Anyway, it's a good thing we know that crazy old wicked witch next door.

BEAR 2:   Yeah, she was able to give us one of her magic potions.

GRUMPY: A magic potion!

SNEEZY: A magic potion!

BEAR 1:   Gee, these two characters must be dumber than dirt. How did they ever get into these stories anyway?

BEAR 2:   I don't know, but I can't wait to hear how Goldy worked her way over to their story—you know, the story about the seven men all with height problems who would spend the whole day working down in a mine and singing to each other.

BEAR 1:   Well, I think I know what happened.

POSSIBLE CONCLUSIONS

1. Goldilocks moves in with the Seven Dwarfs and Snow White wanders through the forest and winds up at the cottage of the Three Bears.

2. Goldilocks asks Big Bad Wolf for directions and then something really terrible happens.

3. Goldilocks goes out on a date with Humpty Dumpty and the entire book of Mother Goose rhymes gets completely scrambled.

4. Goldilocks changes her name to "_____" (name of a currently famous female celebrity), moves to Hollywood, and never speaks to any of the stupid characters in any of the stupid stories ever again.

5. Your idea.

ROBIN HOOD CHANGES HIS STORY AND STEALS FROM THE POOR AND GIVES TO THE RICH

STAGING:

The narrator sits on a stool off to the side of the staging area. The other characters can stand and walk around during the production or be seated on tall stools.

```
         Narrator
            X
                 Robin Hood      Friar Tuck      Little John
                     X               X                X
```

NARRATOR: Once upon a time there was this Robin Hood guy who would walk around the forest all the time dressed up in his green pajamas. He also had a band of merry men who would sing and dance and eat lots of food in the forest along with their pal, Robin Hood. Actually, Robin Hood was more than their pal—he was their leader—which meant that they would do anything he told them to. So one day this band of merry men were sitting around the campfire eating roast warthog or whatever it is that merry men who live in a forest eat, when suddenly Robin Hood had a brilliant thought. Here he is.

ROBIN HOOD: Hi, I'm Robin Hood, the star of this story. You'll notice that I'm good looking, very bright, and live with this gang of merry men here in the deep dark forest. We don't have real jobs—we just do what the storytellers tell us to do—just like characters in those other stories. The only difference is that our story takes place in merry old England a long time ago. So, anyway, one day we were sitting around our campfire waiting for the storytellers to decide what we should be doing when someone got a brilliant idea.

FRIAR TUCK: Well, I was just thinking to myself—you know how in all the other stories the "good guy" or "hero" always does something really nice—like save a princess from the jaws of a fire-breathing dragon or rescue a village of people from a ruthless and evil king or kiss a bunch of slimy frogs to see if any are enchanted princesses.

From *MORE Frantic Frogs and Other Frankly Fractured Folktales for Readers Theatre* by Anthony D. Fredericks. Westport, CT: Teacher Ideas Press. Copyright © 2008.

LITTLE JOHN: By the way, how did I get the name "Little John"? Is it because I have a little head? Is it because I have little feet? Or is it because I have this really little nose that looks like a small raisin on my face?

NARRATOR: Never mind. It's just the name the storytellers gave you. It doesn't mean anything.

LITTLE JOHN: Okay then. Anyway, my buddy Friar Tuck began thinking about all those stories. Then he shared something with us—something we or the storytellers had never thought of before. Why don't we change our story around completely?

ROBIN HOOD: What do you mean?

LITTLE JOHN: Instead of robbing the rich and giving to the poor, why don't we do it the other way around?

FRIAR TUCK: Remember, the idea was mine originally.

ROBIN HOOD: Let me see if I get this right. First we ride out of the woods and into some little village. Then we go into all the homes of the poor people and take all their money and all their possessions. Then we ride out of town and go over to the fancy castles in the development down the road. Then we give all the poor people's money and belongings to the rich people, who are sitting around their swimming pools and drinking iced tea all day.

FRIAR TUCK: Yeah, that's it. But that's not the best part.

POSSIBLE CONCLUSIONS

1. The narrator is really Maid Marion in disguise. She runs to tell the Sheriff of Nottingham (who the heck is he?) about the change in the story, but gets kidnapped by the fire-breathing dragon, who demands a hefty ransom.

2. Robin Hood begins to rob the poor but gets stopped by a posse of wolves, bears, and dwarfs who think that Robin is giving their forest a bad name.

3. A professional storyteller comes over from the nearby Mother Goose book and makes up a new rhyme:

   > Deep inside a forest wood,
   >
   > Lived merry men and Robin Hood.
   >
   > They robbed the poor and saved the rich,
   >
   > Now wasn't that a real strange switch?

4. Somebody sees a poster of Robin Hood in their neighborhood post office and turns him in to the FBI.

5. Your idea.

IF YOU SEE A GINGERBREAD HOUSE IN THE FOREST, DON'T STOP TO NIBBLE—RUN!

STAGING:

The narrators sit on stools off to the side of the staging area. The other characters can stand and walk around during the production or be seated on tall stools.

		Hansel	Gretel	Really Ugly Old Woman	Frog
		X	X	X	X
Narrator 1	Narrator 2				
X	X				

NARRATOR 1: See that Frog character over there [points to Frog]? I'm not sure why a frog is in this story. Somehow he just worked his way into this script. I guess because he saw the title of the book, you know, *MORE Frantic Frogs and Other Frankly Fractured Folktales for Readers Theatre*, he thought that he should have a part in this story.

NARRATOR 2: Yeah, he really shouldn't be in this story at all. He'll probably just mess up the whole story line. So we decided—my friend here [points to other narrator] and I—that this story shouldn't have any frogs. I mean, after all, why would a frog be in a story about a gingerbread house? It just doesn't make sense.

NARRATOR 1: So why don't we all just wave good-bye to the frog [all the characters wave at the Frog].

FROG: Ribbit, Ribbit, Ribbit! [moves off stage]

NARRATOR 2: Now that that's done, let's get on with our story.

NARRATOR 1: First of all, we have to tell you something very, very important.

HANSEL:	Hey, Mr. Fancy Pants narrator person, why don't you let us tell the story? After all, we're the actors around here. You guys are just a bunch of underpaid narrators.
GRETEL:	Yeah, my brother's right. We're the talented actors and actresses in this play. We should tell the story.
NARRATOR 2:	Okay, go ahead and tell your story.
HANSEL:	You see, in another story, my sister Gretel and I were walking through the woods dropping some crumbs along the way. We went deeper and deeper into the deep dark woods.
GRETEL:	Now I'm not sure why the writer of that story thought that we should be roaming around the woods in the middle of the day, but that's what he did. I mean, he could have put us in the middle of a mall, or down at the park, or even at school.
HANSEL:	But no, he thought it would be cool if we were wandering around some deep dark woods. Authors are weird like that, you know.
GRETEL:	So anyway, we were walking through the woods when we came across this gingerbread house. Now I don't know about you, but when I saw a whole house made out of gingerbread, I thought to myself—LET'S PARTY!
HANSEL:	So that's what we did. But that's when the trouble started.
REALLY UGLY OLD WOMAN:	Now I finally get to say something. But first, let me tell you about this gingerbread house I built.

POSSIBLE CONCLUSIONS

1. Really Ugly Old Woman is actually a famous movie actress in disguise. She's always getting arrested for eating small boys and girls.

2. Really Ugly Old Woman is actually a professional wrestler who is looking for some "real action" when along come these two really hungry kids.

3. Hansel is actually Really Ugly Old Woman in disguise. Gretel is actually Frog in disguise. Frog is really the narrator in disguise. Really Ugly Old Woman is actually the author of this book in disguise.

4. Goldilocks walks into this story, and Hansel and Gretel walk over to the Three Bears' house for some good old fashioned porridge.

5. The gingerbread house was built about 20 years ago, which means that the gingerbread is all stale. Nobody wants to eat it; well, except for those Three Blind Mice, who really don't care.

6. Your idea.

APPENDIXES

APPENDIX A: A BIBLIOGRAPHY OF LOTS OF FABLES, TALL TALES, LEGENDS, AND OTHER REALLY COOL STORIES AND BOOKS YOU CAN FIND IN A LIBRARY (or Other Book Place) TO SHARE WITH STUDENTS WHEN THEY'RE LOOKING FOR NEAT STUFF TO READ

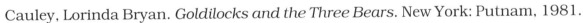

Aesop. *Aesop's Fables.* New York: Viking, 1981.

Alderson, Brian, ed. *Cakes and Custard: Children's Rhymes.* New York: Morrow, 1975.

Andersen, Hans Christian. *Thumbelina.* New York: Dial, 1979.

———. *The Ugly Duckling.* New York: Harcourt Brace Jovanovich, 1979.

Asbjørnsen, Peter Christian, and Jorgen E. Moe. *Three Billy Goats Gruff.* New York: Clarion, 1981.

Brett, Jan. *Beauty and the Beast.* New York: Clarion, 1989.

———. *Goldilocks and the Three Bears.* New York: Dodd, Mead, 1987.

Briggs, Raymond. *The Mother Goose Treasury.* New York: Coward-McCann, 1966.

Brooke, William. *A Telling of the Tales.* New York: Harper & Row, 1990.

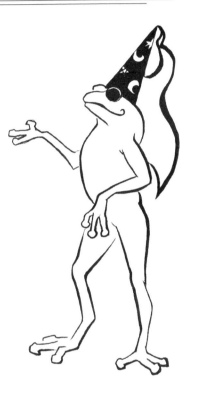

Cauley, Lorinda Bryan. *Goldilocks and the Three Bears.* New York: Putnam, 1981.

———. *The Town Mouse and the Country Mouse.* New York: Putnam, 1984.

Cohn, Amy. *From Sea to Shining Sea: A Treasury of American Folklore and Folk Songs.* New York: Scholastic, 1993.

Cole, Joanna, and Stephanie Calmenson. *Miss Mary Mac: And Other Children's Street Rhymes.* New York: Morrow, 1990.

Craig, Helen. *The Town Mouse and the Country Mouse.* Watertown, MA: Candlewick, 1992.

De Beaumont, Madame Le Prince. *Beauty and the Beast.* New York: Crown, 1986.

De Regniers, Beatrice Schenk. *Red Riding Hood: Retold in Verse.* New York: Atheneum, 1977.

dePaola, Tomie. *The Comic Adventures of Old Mother Hubbard and Her Dog.* San Diego: Harcourt Brace Jovanovich, 1981.

———. *Tomie dePaola's Favorite Nursery Tales.* New York: Putnam, 1986.

———. *Tomie dePaola's Mother Goose.* New York: Putnam, 1985.

Domanska, Janina. *Little Red Hen.* New York: Macmillan, 1973.

Edens, Cooper, ed. *The Glorious Mother Goose.* New York: Atheneum, 1988.

Ehrlich, Amy. *Random House Book of Fairy Tales.* New York: Random, 1985.

Emberley, Barbara. *The Story of Paul Bunyan.* Englewood Cliffs, NJ: Prentice-Hall, 1963.

Evslin, Bernard. *Hercules.* New York: Morrow, 1984.

Fisher, Leonard Everett. *The Olympians: Great Gods and Goddesses of Ancient Greece.* New York: Holiday, 1984.

French, Fiona. *Snow White in New York.* New York: Oxford, 1987.

Galdone, Paul. *Cinderella.* New York: McGraw-Hill, 1978.

———. *The Gingerbread Boy.* New York: Clarion, 1983.

———. *The Hare and the Tortoise.* New York: McGraw-Hill, 1962.

———. *Henny Penny.* New York: Clarion, 1984.

———. *Jack and the Beanstalk.* New York: Clarion, 1982.

———. *Little Bo-Peep.* New York: Clarion, 1982.

———. *The Little Red Hen.* New York: McGraw-Hill, 1985.

———. *Little Red Riding Hood.* New York: McGraw-Hill, 1974.

———. *The Magic Porridge Pot.* New York: Clarion, 1976.

———. *Old Mother Hubbard and Her Dog.* New York: McGraw-Hill, 1960.

———. *Rumpelstiltskin.* New York: Clarion, 1985.

———. *Three Aesop Fox Fables.* New York: Clarion, 1971.

———. *The Three Bears.* New York: Clarion, 1985.

———. *Three Little Kittens.* New York: Clarion, 1986.

———. *The Three Little Pigs.* New York: Clarion, 1984.

Goode, Diane. *Diane Goode's Book of Silly Stories and Songs.* New York: Dutton, 1992.

Greenaway, Kate. *Mother Goose: Or, the Old Nursery Rhymes.* New York: Warne, 1981.

Griego, Morgot C., Betsy L. Bucks, Sharon S. Gilbert, and Laurel H. Kimball. *Tortillas Para Mama and Other Spanish Nursery Rhymes.* New York: Holt, Rinehart & Winston, 1981.

Grimm, Jakob, and Wilhelm Grimm. *The Bremen Town Musicians.* New York: Harper & Row, 1987.

———. *Cinderella.* New York: Greenwillow, 1981.

———. *The Donkey Prince.* New York: Doubleday, 1977.

———. *The Elves and the Shoemaker.* Chicago: Follett, 1967.

———. *Favorite Tales from Grimm.* New York: Four Winds, 1982.

———. *The Frog Prince.* New York: Scholastic, 1987.

———. *Grimm's Fairy Tales: Twenty Stories Illustrated by Arthur Rackham.* New York: Viking, 1973.

———. *Hansel and Gretel.* New York: Morrow, 1980.

———. *Little Red Riding Hood.* New York: Atheneum, 1988.

———. *Popular Folk Tales: The Brothers Grimm.* New York: Doubleday, 1978.

———. *Rapunzel.* New York: Holiday House, 1987.

———. *Rumpelstiltskin.* New York: Four Winds, 1973.

———. *The Shoemaker and the Elves.* New York: Lothrop, 1983.

———. *The Sleeping Beauty.* New York: Atheneum, 1979.

———. *Snow White.* Boston: Little, Brown, 1974.

———. *Snow White and Rose Red.* New York: Delacorte, 1965.

———. *Snow White and the Seven Dwarfs.* New York: Farrar, 1987.

———. *Tom Thumb.* New York: Walck, 1974.

Hague, Michael, ed. *Mother Goose.* New York: Holt, Rinehart & Winston, 1984.

Hale, Sara. *Mary Had a Little Lamb.* New York: Holiday House, 1984.

Haley, Gail. *Jack and the Bean Tree.* New York: Crown, 1986.

Harper, Wilhelmina. *The Gunniwolf.* New York: Dutton, 1967.

Hastings, Selina. *Sir Gawain and the Loathly Lady.* New York: Lothrop, Lee & Shepard, 1985.

Hayes, Sarah. *Bad Egg: The True Story of Humpty Dumpty.* Boston: Little, Brown, 1987.

Hodges, Margaret. *Saint George and the Dragon.* Boston: Little, Brown, 1984.

Huck, Charlotte. *Princess Furball.* New York: Greenwillow, 1989.

Hutchinson, Veronica S. *Henny Penny.* Boston: Little, Brown, 1976.

Hutton, Warwick. *Beauty and the Beast.* New York: Atheneum, 1985.

Ivimey, John W. *The Complete Story of The Three Blind Mice.* New York: Clarion, 1987.

Jacobs, Joseph. *Jack and the Beanstalk.* New York: Putnam, 1983.

———. *The Three Little Pigs.* New York: Atheneum, 1980.

Jeffers, Susan. *If Wishes Were Horses: Mother Goose Rhymes.* New York: Dutton, 1979.

Kellogg, Steven. *Chicken Little.* New York: Morrow, 1985.

———. *Johnny Appleseed.* New York: Morrow, 1988.

———. *Mike Fink.* New York: Morrow, 1992.

———. *Paul Bunyan.* New York: Morrow, 1974.

———. *Pecos Bill.* New York: Morrow, 1986.

Kimmel, Eric. *The Gingerbread Man.* New York: Holiday, 1993.

Kingsley, Charles. *The Heroes.* New York: Mayflower, 1980.

Lobel, Arnold. *Gregory Griggs and Other Nursery Rhyme People.* New York: Greenwillow, 1978

———. *The Random House Book of Mother Goose.* New York: Random House, 1986.

Marshall, James. *Goldilocks and the Three Bears.* New York: Dial, 1988.

———. *Hansel and Gretel.* New York: Dial, 1990.

———. *James Marshall's Mother Goose.* New York: Farrar, Straus & Giroux, 1979.

———. *Red Riding Hood.* New York: Dial, 1987.

Martin, Sarah. *The Comic Adventures of Old Mother Hubbard and Her Dog.* San Diego: Harcourt Brace, 1981.

McKinley, Robin. *The Outlaws of Sherwood.* New York: Greenwillow, 1988.

Miles, Bernard. *Robin Hood: His Life and Legend.* New York: Hamlyn, 1979.

Miller, Mitchell. *One Misty Moisty Morning.* New York: Farrar, Straus & Giroux, 1971.

Newbery, John. *The Original Mother Goose's Melody.* New York: Gale, 1969.

Opie, Iona, and Peter Opie. *A Nursery Companion.* London: Oxford University Press, 1980.

———. *The Oxford Nursery Rhyme Book.* London: Oxford University Press, 1984.

———. *Tail Feathers from Mother Goose: The Opie Rhyme Book.* Boston: Little, Brown, 1988.

Ormerod, Jan. *The Story of Chicken Licken.* New York: Lothrop, 1986.

Oxenbury, Helen. *The Helen Oxenbury Nursery Story Book.* New York: Knopf, 1985.

Pearson, Tracey. *Old Macdonald Had a Farm.* New York: Dial, 1984.

Perrault, Charles. *Cinderella.* New York: Dial, 1985.

———. *Little Red Riding Hood.* New York: Scholastic, 1971.

———. *Puss in Boots.* New York: Clarion, 1976.

———. *The Sleeping Beauty*. New York: Viking, 1972.

Provensen, Alice, and Martin Provensen. *Old Mother Hubbard*. New York: Random House, 1982.

Riordan, James. *Tales of King Arthur*. New York: Rand McNally, 1982.

Rounds, Glen. *Old Macdonald Has a Farm*. New York, Holiday House, 1989.

———. *Three Little Pigs and The Big Bad Wolf*. New York: Holiday, 1992.

Scieszka, Jon. *The Stinky Cheese Man and Other Fairly Stupid Tales*. New York: Viking, 1992.

———. *The True Story of the 3 Little Pigs*. New York: Viking, 1989.

Southey, Robert. *The Three Bears*. New York: Putnam, 1984.

Spier, Peter. *London Bridge is Falling Down*. New York: Doubleday, 1967.

Stevens, Janet. *Goldilocks and the Three Bears*. New York: Holiday House, 1986.

———. *The House That Jack Built*. New York: Holiday House, 1985.

———. *The Tortoise and the Hare*. New York: Holiday House, 1984.

———. *The Town Mouse and the Country Mouse*. New York: Holiday House, 1987.

Still, James. *Jack and the Wonder Beans*. New York: Putnam, 1977.

Stoutenburg, Adrien. *American Tall Tales*. New York: Viking, 1966.

Tarrant, Margaret. *Nursery Rhymes*. New York: Crowell, 1978.

Thompson, Pat, ed. *Rhymes Around the Day*. New York: Lothrop, Lee & Shepard, 1983.

Tripp, Wallace. *Granfa' Grig Had a Pig and Other Rhymes Without Reason from Mother Goose*. Boston: Little, Brown, 1976.

Tudor, Tasha. *Mother Goose*. New York: Walck, 1972.

Watson, Wendy. *Wendy Watson's Mother Goose*. New York: Lothrop, Lee & Shepard, 1989.

Watts, Bernadette. *Goldilocks and the Three Bears*. New York: Holt, Rinehart & Winston, 1985.

Wildsmith, Brian. *Brian Wildsmith's Mother Goose*. New York: Oxford University Press, 1982.

Willard, Nancy. *Beauty and the Beast*. New York: Harcourt Brace Jovanovich, 1992.

Zemach, Harve. *Duffy and the Devil*. New York: Farrar, Straus & Giroux, 1973

Zuromskis, Diane. *The Farmer in the Dell*. Boston: Little, Brown, 1978.

APPENDIX B: THIS IS SOOOOOOO INCREDIBLE! HERE'S A GREAT BIG PILE OF WEIRD, WACKY, AND WILD READERS THEATRE TITLES KIDS CAN USE TO CREATE THEIR OWN ORIGINAL READERS THEATRE SCRIPTS JUST LIKE THE AUTHOR OF THIS BOOK DID (and How Cool Is That?)

1. Our Teacher Is the Most Beautiful and Most Intelligent Person in the Entire World (and/or Universe)

2. Our Teacher Marries a Rich and Handsome Prince (Who Just Happens to Eat Flies)

3. Our Teacher Never, Never, Ever, Ever Gives Math Homework Again!

4. Mother Goose Is Really a Duck (or Maybe a Really Strange Crow)

5. "Don't You Dare Touch My Foot," Cinderella Yelled at the Handsome Prince

6. Mary Had a Little Octopus (She Couldn't Find Her Lamb)

7. Sleeping Beauty Never Wakes Up (She Just Keeps Snoring for About a Thousand Years or So)

8. The Three Billy Goats Gruff Get an Attitude Adjustment

9. Thumbelina and Tom Thumb are Not Really Twins, They Just Have Funny Sounding Names

10. Red Riding Hood, Green Jumping Cape, and Blue Trotting Coat Teach the Wolf a Lesson He'll Never Forget

11. Hansel and Gretel Change Their Names and Become Finalists on American Idol®.

12. The Three Bears Move Out of the Cottage and into a Condo in the City

13. Little Miss Muffet Goes Berserk and Starts Beating Up all the Insects in the Forest

14. The Enchanted Prince Gets Kissed by the Evil Witch and Changes His Life Forever

15. Paul Bunyan Stubs His Toe on Chicago and Starts to Cry

16. Chicken Little Gets Fried for Dinner

17. The Prince Finds Cinderella's Glass Slipper and Boy, Does It Stink!

18. Mary Had a Little Lamb, a Little Turkey, a Little Chicken, and a Little Roast Beef—and She Was Still Hungry!

19. The Tortoise and the Hare Fall in Love (Hint: It's Not Pretty!)

20. Goldilocks Goes on Trial for Breaking and Entering

21. Sleeping Beauty and the Giant Squid

22. A Stack of Pancakes, Two Sausage Links, Orange Juice, Buttered Toast, and Humpty Dumpty on the Side

23. Baa Baa Black Sheep; Neigh Neigh Orange Horse; Woof Woof Purple Dog, Meow Meow Crimson Cat

24. The Three Blind Mice Go to the Optometrist and Get Some Really Cool Glasses

25. Why the Heck Do We Keep Going Round and Round the Stupid Mulberry Bush?

26. Little Miss Muffet Eats a Whole Lot of Snickers Bars 'Cause She Just Doesn't Like Curds and Whey Anymore

27. This Little Piggy Said, "I'm Really Tired of Going Wee-Wee-Wee All Day Long!"

28. Little Jack Horner Sat in a Corner Eating Some Cheese Whiz®

29. Jack Climbs to the Top of the Beanstalk and Sees Something Really Disgusting

30. Snow White Redecorates Peter Pumpkin-Eater's House

31. The Three Billy Goats Gruff Start Dating the Three Little Pigs

32. One, Two, Buckle My Shoe; Three, Four, Our Teacher Can Snore!

33. Cinderella: Worldwide Wrestling Champion!

34. Little Boy Blue Marries Little Red Riding Hood and Little Purple Baby Is Born

35. Old King Cole Decided He Wasn't Merry Anymore

36. Rumpelstiltskin Changes His Name to Bill (or Sam or Tom or Ken)

37. Roses Are Red, Violets Are Blue, Our Teacher is Very, Very Crazy, and So Are You

38. Mary Had a Little Lamb, Who Grew Up to Become a Very Bad Sheep with an Attitude Problem

39. Georgie Porgie, Pudding and Pie, Kissed the Girls and Got into a Lot of Trouble with the Principal

40. Beauty and the Beast Get Married and Honeymoon in Hawaii

41. The Ugly Duckling Enters a Beauty Pageant (Hint: It's not a pretty story)

42. Rapunzel Starts Losing Her Hair

43. Paul Bunyan Gets Really Hungry and Eats Denver

44. Dragons Are Just Alligators with a Hormone Problem

45. Alice in Wonderland Starts Teaching Fourth Grade

46. The Emperor Gets All His New Clothes at Wal-Mart

47. The Frog Prince Starts Pumping Iron (Watch Out!)

48. The Evil Stepmother Finally Figures Out Why Nobody Likes Her

49. The Goose That Laid the Golden Egg Is Really a Porcupine in Disguise

50. Jack Grows Some Sweet Peas, Carrots, and Broccoli Instead of a Beanstalk

51. Peter Pan Gets Arrested for Flying Over the White House

52. Pinocchio Gets a Nose Job

53. The Seven Dwarfs Star in a New Pirate Movie.

54. "Kiss My Slime, Toadface!"

55. A "Once Upon a Time" Story That Really Happened

56. If You Think the Fire-Breathing Dragon is Bad, Wait Till You See Our Teacher

57. How to Barbeque the Three Little Pigs—Hints for the Busy Cook

58. Jack and Jill Hurt Themselves Really Bad

59. Our Principal—A True Prince Charming

60. Donald Gets in Touch with His Inner Duck

61. Watch Out! The Wolves Are in Town.

62. The Cafeteria Lady Is Really a Wicked Witch Who Eats Children

63. "Short Men are Real Slobs," Snow White Mutters One Day

64. The Three Bears All Fail Fifth Grade

APPENDIX C: RESOURCES AND OTHER THINGS AUTHORS ALWAYS PUT AT THE END OF A BOOK (But That Doesn't Mean They're Not Important)

READERS THEATRE BOOKS

Barchers, S. *Fifty Fabulous Fables: Beginning Readers Theatre.* Westport, CT: Teacher Ideas Press, 1997.

———. *From Atalanta to Zeus.* Westport, CT: Teacher Ideas Press, 2001.

———. *Judge for Yourself.* Westport, CT: Teacher Ideas Press, 2004.

———. *Multicultural Folktales: Readers Theatre for Elementary Students.* Westport, CT: Teacher Ideas Press, 2000.

———. *Readers Theatre for Beginning Readers.* Westport, CT: Teacher Ideas Press, 1993.

———. *Scary Readers Theatre.* Westport, CT: Teachers Ideas Press, 1994.

Barchers, S., and J. L. Kroll. *Classic Readers Theatre for Young Adults.* Westport, CT: Teacher Ideas Press, 2002.

Barchers, S., and C. R. Pfeffinger. *More Readers Theatre for Beginning Readers.* Westport, CT: Teacher Ideas Press, 2006.

Barnes, J. W. *Sea Songs.* Westport, CT: Teacher Ideas Press, 2004.

Black, A. N. *Born Storytellers.* Westport, CT: Teacher Ideas Press, 2005.

Criscoe, B. L., and P. J. Lanasa. *Fairy Tales for Two Readers.* Westport, CT: Teacher Ideas Press, 1995.

Dixon, N., A. Davies, and C. Politano. *Learning with Readers Theatre: Building Connections.* Winnipeg, Canada: Peguis Publishers, 1996.

Fredericks, A. D. *Frantic Frogs and Other Frankly Fractured Folktales for Readers Theatre.* Westport, CT: Teacher Ideas Press, 1993.

———. *Mother Goose Readers Theatre for Beginning Readers.* Westport, CT: Teacher Ideas Press, 2007.

———. *Nonfiction Readers Theatre for Beginning Readers.* Westport, CT: Teacher Ideas Press, 2007.

———. *Readers Theatre for American History.* Westport, CT: Teacher Ideas Press, 2001.

———. *Science Fiction Readers Theatre.* Westport, CT: Teacher Ideas Press, 2002.

———. *Silly Salamanders and Other Slightly Stupid Stories for Readers Theatre.* Westport, CT: Teacher Ideas Press, 2000.

———. *Songs and Rhymes Readers Theatre for Beginning Readers.* Westport, CT: Teacher Ideas Press, 2007.

———. *Tadpole Tales and Other Totally Terrific Treats for Readers Theatre.* Westport, CT: Teacher Ideas Press, 1997.

Garner, J. *Wings of Fancy: Using Readers Theatre to Study Fantasy Genre.* Westport, CT: Teacher Ideas Press, 2006

Georges, C., and C. Cornett. *Reader's Theatre.* Buffalo, NY: D.O.K. Publishers, 1990.

Haven, K. *Great Moments in Science: Experiments and Readers Theatre.* Westport, CT: Teacher Ideas Press, 1996.

Jenkins, D. R. *Just Deal with It.* Westport, CT: Teacher Ideas Press, 2004.

Johnson, T. D., and D. R. Louis. *Bringing It All Together: A Program for Literacy.* Portsmouth, NH: Heinemann, 1990.

Kroll, J. L. *Simply Shakespeare.* Westport, CT: Teacher Ideas Press, 2003.

Latrobe, K. H., C. Casey, and L. A. Gann. *Social Studies Readers Theatre for Young Adults.* Westport, CT: Teacher Ideas Press, 1991.

Laughlin, M. K., P. T. Black, and K. H. Latrobe. *Social Studies Readers Theatre for Children.* Westport, CT: Teacher Ideas Press, 1991.

Laughlin, M. K., and K. H. Latrobe. *Readers Theatre for Children.* Westport, CT: Teacher Ideas Press, 1990.

Martin, J. M. *12 Fabulously Funny Fairy Tale Plays.* New York: Instructor Books, 2002.

Peterson, C. *Around the World Through Holidays.* Westport, CT: Teacher Ideas Press, 2005.

Pfeffinger, C. R. *Character Counts.* Westport, CT: Teacher Ideas Press, 2003.

———. *Holiday Readers Theatre.* Westport, CT: Teacher Ideas Press, 1994.

Pugliano-Martin, C. *25 Just-Right Plays for Emergent Readers (Grades K–1).* New York: Scholastic, 1999.

Shepard, A. *Folktales on Stage: Children's Plays for Readers Theatre.* Olympia, WA: Shepard Publications, 2003.

———. *Readers on Stage: Resources for Readers Theatre.* Olympia, WA: Shepard Publications, 2004.

———. *Stories on Stage: Children's Plays for Readers Theatre.* Olympia, WA: Shepard Publications, 2005.

Sloyer, S. *From the Page to the Stage.* Westport, CT: Teacher Ideas Press, 2003.

Smith, C. *Extraordinary Women from U.S. History.* Westport, CT: Teacher Ideas Press, 2003.

Wolf, J. M. *Cinderella Outgrows the Glass Slipper and Other Zany Fractured Fairy Tale Plays.* New York: Scholastic, 2002.

Wolfman, J. *How and Why Stories for Readers Theatre.* Westport, CT: Teacher Ideas Press, 2004.

Worthy, J. *Readers Theatre for Building Fluency: Strategies and Scripts for Making the Most of This Highly Effective, Motivating, and Research-Based Approach to Oral Reading.* New York: Scholastic, 2005.

WEB SITES

http://www.aaronshep.com/rt/RTE.html. How to use readers theatre, sample scripts from a children's author who specializes in readers theatre, and an extensive list of resources.

http://www.cdli.ca/CITE/langrt.htm. This site has lots of information, covering what readers theatre is, readers theatre scripts, writing scripts, recommended print resources, and recommended online resources.

http://www.teachingheart.net/readerstheater.htm. Here you'll discover lots of plays and scripts to print and read in your classroom or library.

http://literacyconnections.com/readerstheater. There is an incredible number of resources and scripts at this all-inclusive site.

http://www.proteacher.com/070173.shmtl. This site is a growing collection of tens of thousands of ideas shared by teachers across the United States and around the world.

http://www.readerstheatredigest.com. This is an online magazine of ideas, scripts, and teaching strategies.

http://www.readerstheatre.escd.net. This site has over 150 small poems, stories, and chants for readers theatre.

http://www.storycart.com. Storycart Press's subscription service provides an inexpensive opportunity to have timely scripts delivered to teachers or librarians each month. Each script is created or adapted by well-known writer Suzanne Barchers, author of several readers theatre books (see above).

PROFESSIONAL ORGANIZATION

Institute for Readers Theatre
P.O. Box 421262
San Diego, CA 92142
(858) 277-4274
www.readerstheatreinstitute.com

INDEX

ABOUT THE AUTHOR GUY WHO WROTE THIS BOOK
(Careful, He Eats Flies)

Anthony D. Fredericks (afredericks60@comcast.net). There will undoubtedly be many sharp-eyed readers who are now saying, "You know, I can see why he loves frogs so much—he looks sorta . . . well . . . he looks sorta . . . amphibious!" Of course, through the clever use of a certain software package we've been able to put a human face on him, plop some glasses on his nose, give him a full head of hair, and take at least two decades off his age (in frog-years, he's actually 487 years old). Nevertheless, it should be quite obvious that this author guy is no enchanted prince. He does, however, have that incessant smile plastered on his face—but so do a lot of insurance salesmen and used car dealers.

Here's some stuff we do know about Tony: His background includes more than 35 years of experience as a classroom teacher, reading specialist, curriculum coordinator, staff developer, professional storyteller, and college professor. He is a prolific author, having written more than 65 teacher resource books, including the enormously popular *Frantic Frogs and Other Frankly Fractured Folktales for Readers Theatre*, the best-selling *Guided Reading in Grades 3–6*, the celebrated *Much More Social Studies Through Children's Literature*, and the dynamic *Investigating Natural Disasters Through Children's Literature*. In addition, he's authored more than three dozen award-winning children's books, including *The Tsunami Quilt: Grandfather's Story, Near One Cattail: Turtles, Logs and Leaping Frogs, Dinosaur Droppings, Animal Sharpshooters*, and *A Is for Anaconda: A Rainforest Alphabet Book*.

Tony currently teaches elementary methods courses in reading, language arts, science, social studies, and children's literature at York College in York, Pennsylvania (where his undergraduate students have other names for him besides "amphibian"). He is also a popular and enthusiastic visiting children's author to elementary schools throughout North America, where he celebrates writing with a new generation of young authors. During his school visits he is well-prepared to answer the four most-asked questions of every children's author: (1) "Where do you get your ideas?" (2) "How much money do you make?" (3) "How old are you?" and (4) "Is your wife pretty?"